EDITORIAL

In the name of liberty...

A new generation of democratic leaders is actively eroding essential freedoms, says
Rachael Jolley

48(04): 1/3 | DOI: 10.1177/0306422019895763

LIKE BROTHERS IN arms, they revel in the same set of characteristics. They share them, and their favourite ways of using them, on social media.

From Orbán to Trump and from Bolsonaro to Johnson, national leaders who want to dismiss analysis with a personalised tweet, and never want to answer a direct question, have come to power – and are using power to silence us. They like to think of themselves as strongmen but what, in fact, they are doing is channelling the worst kind of machismo.

For toughness, read intolerance of disagreement. They are extremely uncomfortable with public criticism. They would rather hold a Facebook "press conference" where they are not pressed than one where reporters get to push them on details they would rather not address. Despite running countries, they try to pretend that those who hold them to account are the elite who the public should not trust.

While every generation has its "tough" leaders, what's different about today's is that they are everywhere, and learning, copying and sharing their measures with each other – aided, of course, by the internet, which is their ultimate best friend. And this is not just a phenomenon we are seeing on one continent. Right now these techniques are coming at us from all around the globe, as if one giant algorithm is showing them the way. And it's not happening just in countries run by unelected dictators; democratically elected leaders are very firmly part of this boys' club.

Here are some favoured techniques:

If you don't like some media coverage, you look at ways of closing down or silencing that media outlet, and possibly others. Could a friend buy it? Could you bring in some legislation that shuts it out? How about making sure it loses its advertising? That is happening now. In Hungary, there are very few independent media outlets left, and the media that remain is pretty scared about what might happen to them. Hungarian journalists are moving to other countries to get the chance to write about the issues. In China, President Xi Jinping has just increased the pressure on journalists who report for official outlets by insisting they take a knowledge test, which is very much like a loyalty test (see p.11), before being given press cards. Just today, as I sit here writing, I've switched on the radio to hear that the UK's Conservative Party has made an official complaint to the TV watchdog over Channel 4's coverage of the general election campaign (there was a debate last night on climate change where party leaders who didn't turn up →

EDITOR-IN-CHIEF
Rachael Jolley
DEPUTY EDITOR
Jemimah Steinfeld
SUB EDITORS
Tracey Bagshaw,
Adam Aiken

CONTRIBUTING EDITORS
Jan Fox (USA),
Kaya Genç (Turkey),
Laura Silvia Battaglia
(Yemen and Iraq),
Stephen Woodman
(Mexico)

EDITORIAL ASSISTANT
Orna Herr
ART DIRECTOR
Matthew Hasteley
COVER
Ben Jennings

THANKS TO
Ryan McChrystal

MAGAZINE PRINTED BY
Page Bros.,
Norwich UK

Supported by
ARTS COUNCIL ENGLAND

INDEX ON CENSORSHIP
indexoncensorship.org | +44 (0) 20 3848 9820 | 1 Rivington Place, London EC2A 3BA, United Kingdom

→ were replaced with giant blocks of ice). A party source told the Conservative-supporting Daily Telegraph newspaper: "If we are re-elected, we will have to review Channel 4's public service broadcasting obligations. Any review would, of course, look at whether its remit should be better focused so it is serving the public in the best way possible." In summary, they are saying they will close down the media that disagree with them.

This not very veiled threat is very much in line with the rhetoric from President Donald Trump in the USA and President Viktor Orbán in Hungary about the media knowing its place as more a subservient hat-tipping servant than a watchdog holding power to account. It's also not so far from attitudes that are prevalent in Russia and China about the role of the media.

For those who might think that media freedom is a luxury, or doesn't have much importance in their lives, I suggest they take a quick look at any country or point in history where media freedom was taken away, and then ask themselves: "Do I want to live there?"

Dictators know that control of the message underpins their power, and so does this generation of macho leaders. Getting the media "under control" is a high priority. Trump went on the offensive against journalists from the first minute he strode out on to the public stage. Brazil's newish leader, President Jair Bolsonaro, knows it too. In fact, he got together with Trump on the steps of the White House to agree on a fightback against "fake news", and we all should know what they mean right there. "Fake news" is news they don't like and really would rather not hear.

New York Times deputy general counsel David McCraw told Index that this was "a very dark moment for press freedom worldwide" (see p.20).

When the founders of the USA sat down to write the Constitution – that essential document of freedom, written because many of them had fled from countries where they were not allowed to speak, take certain jobs or practise their religion – they had in mind creating a country where freedom was protected. The First Amendment encapsulates the right to criticise the powerful, but now the country is led by someone who says, basically, he doesn't support it. No wonder McCraw feels a deep sense of unease.

But when Trump's team started to try to control media coverage, by not inviting the most critical media to press briefings, what was impressive was that American journalists from across the political spectrum spoke out for media freedom. When then White House press secretary Sean Spicer tried to stop journalists from The New York Times, The Guardian and CNN from attending some briefings, Bret Baier, a senior anchor with Fox News, spoke out. He said on Twitter: "Some at CNN & NYT stood w/FOX News when the Obama admin attacked us & tried 2 exclude us-a WH gaggle should be open to all credentialed orgs."

The media stood up and criticised the attempt to allow only favoured outlets access, with many (including The Wall Street Journal, AP and Bloomberg) calling it out. What was impressive was that they were standing up for the principle of media freedom. The White House is likely to at least think carefully about similar moves when it realises it risks alienating its friendly media as well as its critics.

And that's the lesson for media everywhere. Don't let them divide and rule you. If a newspaper that you think of as the opposition is not allowed access to a press briefing because the prime minister or the president doesn't like it, you should be shouting about it just as hard as if it happened to you, because it is about the principle. If you don't believe in the principle, in time they will come for you and no one will be there to speak out.

That's the big point being made by Baier: it happened to us and people spoke up for us, so now I am doing the same. A seasoned Turkish journalist told me that one of the reasons the

---

And that's the lesson for media everywhere. Don't let them divide and rule you

LEFT: Political reporter for the Daily Mirror Nicola Bartlett beside the Conservative party campaign bus, on which she was refused a place

Again in Hungary, people are put into the "outsiders" box if they are gay, women who haven't had children or don't conform to the ideas that the Orbán government stands for.

Dividing people into "them and us" has huge implications for our democracies. In separating people, we start to lose our empathy for people who are "other" and we potentially stop standing up for them when something happens. It creates divides that are useful for those in power to manipulate to their advantage.

The University of Birmingham's Henriette van der Bloom recently co-published research pamphlet Crisis of Rhetoric: Renewing Political Speech and Speechwriting. She said: "I think there is a risk we are all putting ourselves and others into boxes, then we cannot really collaborate about improving our society. Some would say that is what is partly going on at the moment." Looking forward, she saw one impact could be "a society in crisis, speeches are delivered, and people listen, but it becomes more and more polarising".

But it's not just the future, it's today. We already see societies in crisis, with democratic values being threatened and eroded. This does not point to a rosy future. But there are some signs for optimism. In this issue, we also feature protesters who have campaigned and achieved significant change. In Romania, a mass weekly protest against a new law which would allow political corruption has ended with the government standing down; in Hungary, a new opposition mayor has been elected in Budapest.

Democracies need to remember that criticism and political opposition are an essential part of their success. We must hope they do. ⊗

Rachael Jolley is editor-in-chief of Index on Censorship

Turkish government led by President Recep Tayyip Erdogan was able to get away with restrictions on critical media early on, was because the liberal media hadn't stood up for the principle in earlier years when conservative press outlets were being excluded or criticised.

Sadly, the UK media did not show many signs of standing united when, during this year's general election campaign, the Daily Mirror, a Labour-supporting newspaper, was kicked off the Conservative Party's campaign "battle bus". The bus carries journalists and Prime Minister Boris Johnson around the country during the campaign. The Mirror, which has about 11 million readers, was the only newspaper not allowed to board the bus. When the Mirror's political editor called on other media to boycott the bus, the reaction was muted. Conservative Party tacticians will have seen this as a success, given the lack of solidarity to this move by the rest of the media (unlike the US coverage of the White House incident).

The lesson here is to stand up for the principles of freedom and democracy all the time, not just when they affect you. If you don't, they will be gone before you know it.

Rallying rhetoric is another tried and tested tactic. They use it to divide the public into "them and us", and try to convert others to thinking they are "people like us". If we, the public, think they are on our side, we are more likely to put the X in their ballot box. Trump and Orbán practise the "people like us" and "everyone else is our enemy" strategies with abandon. They rail against people they don't like using words such as "traitor".

CONTENTS

VOLUME 48 NUMBER 04 – WINTER 2019

1 IN THE NAME OF LIBERTY... RACHAEL JOLLEY
Our freedoms are being taken before our very eyes

THE BIG NOISE

How macho leaders hide their weakness by stiffling dissent, debate and democracy

8 WILL THE REAL XI JINPING PLEASE STAND UP? JEFFREY WASSERSTROM
China's most powerful leader since Mao wears many hats - some of them draconian

12 CHALLENGING ORBÁN'S ECHO CHAMBER VIKTÓRIA SERDÜLT
Against the odds a new mayor from an opposition party has come to power in Budapest. We report on his promises to push back against Orbán

15 TAKING ON THE LION STEFANO POZZEBON
With an aggressive former army captain as president, Brazilian journalists are having to employ bodyguards to stay safe. But they're fighting back

18 SEVEN TIPS FOR CRUSHING FREE SPEECH IN THE 21ST CENTURY ROB SEARS
Hey big guy, we know you're the boss man, but here are some tips to really rule the roost

20 "MEDIA MUST COME TOGETHER"
RACHAEL JOLLEY AND JAN FOX
Interview with the New York Times' lawyer on why the media needs to rally free speech. Plus Trump vs. former presidents, the ultimate machometer

24 TOOLS OF THE REAL TECHNOS
MARK FRARY
The current autocrats have technology bent to their every whim. We're vulnerable and exposed

27 MODI AND HIS ANGRY MEN
SOMAK GHOSHAL
India's men are responding with violence to Modi's increasingly nationalist war cry

30 GLOBAL LEADERS SMEAR THEIR CRITICS CAROLINE LEES
Dissenters beware - these made-up charges are being used across borders to distract and destroy

33 SEXISM IS PRESIDENT'S POWER TOOL MIRIAM GRACE GO
Duterte is using violent language and threats against journalists, Rappler's news editor explains

36 STRIPSEARCH MARTIN ROWSON
Putin, Trump, Bolsonora - macho or... nacho?

38 SOUNDS AGAINST SILENCE KAYA GENÇ
Far from a bad rap here as Turkey's leading musicians use music to criticise the government

CREDIT: Ben Jennings

41 UN-MENTIONABLES ORNA HERR

The truths these world leaders really can't handle

42 SALVINI EXPLOITS "LACK OF TRUST" IN ITALIAN MEDIA ALESSIO PERRONE

The reputation of Italian media is poor, which plays straight into the hands of the far-right politician

45 MACHO, MACHO MAN NEEMA KOMBA

A toxic form of masculinity has infected politics in Tanzania. Democracy is on the line

48 PUTIN'S PUSHBACKS ANDREY ARKHANGELSKIY

Russians signed up for prosperity not oppression. Is Putin failing to deliver his side of the deal?

50 TRYING TO SHUT DOWN WOMEN JODIE GINSBERG

Women are being forced out of politics as a result of abuse. We need to rally behind them, for all our sakes

IN FOCUS

54 DIRTY INDUSTY, DIRTY TACTICS STEPHEN WOODMAN

Miners in Brazil, Mexico and Peru are going to extremes to stop those who are trying to protest

57 MUSIC TO YEMEN'S EARS LAURA SILVIA BATTAGLIA

Could a new orchestra in Yemen signal the end of oppressive Houthi rule? These women hope so

61 PLAY ON JEMIMAH STEINFELD

The darling of the opera scene, Jamie Barton, and the woman behind a hit refugee orchestra, discuss taboo breaking on stage

64 THE FINAL CHAPTER? KAROLINE KAN

The closing of Beijing's iconic Bookworm has been met with cries of sadness around the world. Why?

66 WORKING IT OUT STEVEN BOROWIEC

An exclusive interview about workplace bullying with the Korean Air steward who was forced to kneel and apologise for not serving nuts correctly

69 PROTEST WORKS RACHAEL JOLLEY AND JEMIMAH STEINFELD

Two activists on how their protest movements led to real political change in Hungary and Romania

73 IT'S A LITTLE BIT SILENT, THIS FEELING INSIDE SILVIA NORTES

Spain's historic condemnation of suicide is contributing to a damaging culture of silence today

CULTURE

78 HONG KONG WRITES TAMMY LAI-MING HO

A Hong Kong poet talks to Index from the frontline of the protests about how her writing keeps her and others going. Also one of her poems published here

80 WRITING TO THE CHALLENGE KAYA GENÇ

Orna Herr speaks to the Turkish author about his new short story, written exclusively for the magazine, in which Turkish people get obsessed with raccoons

86 PLAYING THE JOKER JONATHAN TEL

The award-winning writer tells Rachael Jolley about the power of subversive jokes. Plus an exclusive short story set in a Syrian prison

94 GOING GRAPHIC ANDALUSIA KNOLL SOLOFF AND MARCO PARRA

Being a journalist in Mexico is often a deadly pursuit. But sometimes the horrors of this reality are only shown in cartoon form, as the journalist and illustrator show

98 GOVERNMENTS SEEK TO CONTROL REPORTS ORNA HERR

Journalists are facing threats from all angles, including new terrorist legislation

101 CULTURE VULTURES JEMIMAH STEINFELD

The extent of art censorship in democracies is far greater than initially meets the eye, Index reveals

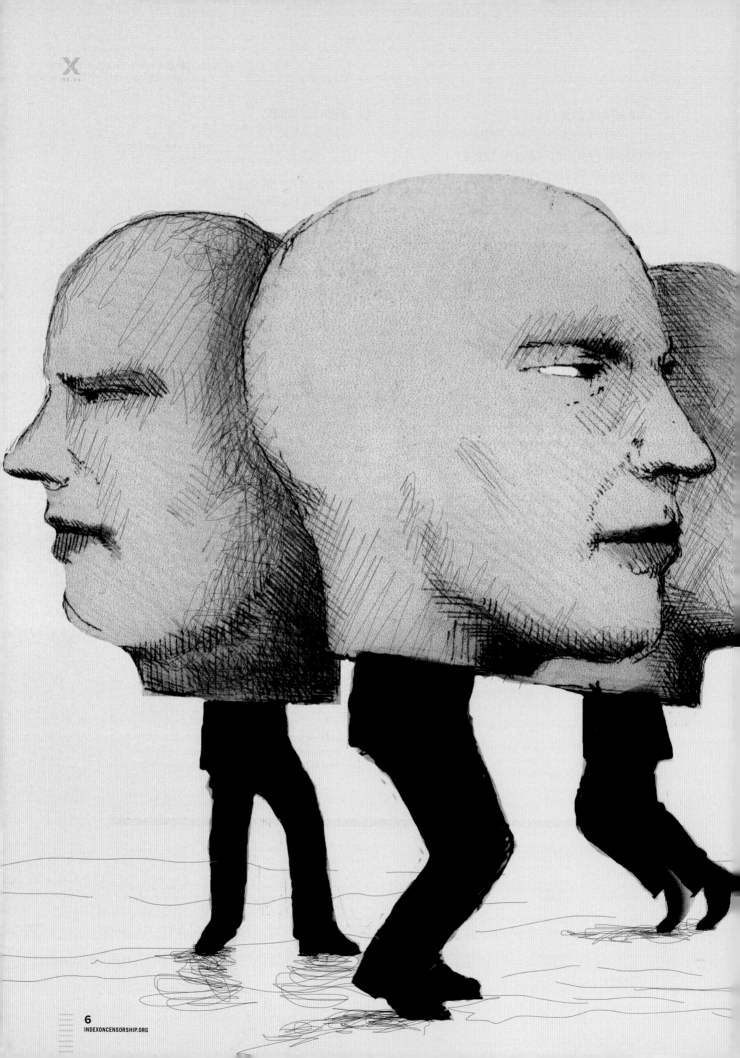

SPECIAL
REPORT

 THE BIG NOISE: How macho leaders hide
their weakness by stifling dissent, debate
and democracy

08   **WILL THE REAL XI JINPING PLEASE STAND UP?** JEFFREY WASSERSTROM

12   **CHALLENGING ORBÁN'S ECHO CHAMBER** VIKTÓRIA SERDÜLT

15   **TAKING ON THE LION** STEFANO POZZEBON

18   **SEVEN TIPS FOR CRUSHING FREE SPEECH IN THE 21ST CENTURY** ROB SEARS

20   **"MEDIA MUST COME TOGETHER"** RACHAEL JOLLEY AND JAN FOX

24   **TOOLS OF THE REAL TECHNOS** MARK FRARY

27   **MODI AND HIS ANGRY MEN** SOMAK GHOSHAL

30   **GLOBAL LEADERS SMEAR THEIR CRITICS** CAROLINE LEES

33   **SEXISM IS PRESIDENT'S POWER TOOL** MIRIAM GRACE GO

36   **STRIPSEARCH** MARTIN ROWSON

38   **SOUNDS AGAINST SILENCE** KAYA GENÇ

41   **UN-MENTIONABLES** ORNA HERR

42   **SALVINI EXPLOITS "LACK OF TRUST" IN ITALIAN MEDIA** ALESSIO PERRONE

45   **MACHO, MACHO MAN** NEEMA KOMBA

48   **PUTIN'S PUSHBACKS** ANDREY ARKHANGELSKIY

Will the real Xi Jinping please stand up?

Nicknamed the Chairman of Everything, China's most powerful leader since Mao channels many different traits, writes **Jeffrey Wasserstrom**

48(04): 8/11 I DOI: 10.1177/0306422019895699

THERE'S A MAN named Xi Jinping who lives in Beijing but often travels. When on the road, he talks of his love of foreign novelists and respect for international institutions and accords. When in the USA, he said he was a Hemingway fan. In France, he expressed his regard for Montesquieu, Molière, Montaigne and Maupassant (as well as various local writers whose surnames don't begin with "M"). He defends the Paris Climate Agreement and, in 2017, he made a good impression at Davos. Sporting the same type of jacket and tie as many male attendees, he quoted Dickens and gave what Reuters described as a "vigorous defence of free trade".

There is another man named Xi Jinping, however, who is different. While he, too, sometimes wears a jacket and tie, he prefers to don military fatigues or put on what Westerners call a "Mao suit". He is not a globalist and insists that his country's young people need to be protected from the polluting influence of Western ideas. He dismissed a Hague Court ruling against Beijing regarding the South China Seas islands as an effort to infringe on China's sovereignty. He has no patience for international criticism of human-rights abuses in Xinjiang or praise for the Dalai Lama and Hong Kong protesters. He sees these as proof that the foreign powers responsible for what Chinese textbooks call a "century of humiliation" – which lasted from the 1840s until the 1940s and saw the country bullied by the USA and invaded by European and Japanese soldiers – are determined to block China's rightful rise.

In thinking about these two personas, it's worth remembering that the clout of Xi, the most powerful Chinese leader since Mao Zedong and Deng Xiaoping, derives from two posts. Early in 2013, he became head of state. But he was already China's most powerful person because he headed something else – the communist party. He became the Chinese Communist Party's chief late in 2012, and, domestically, that's still his most important post.

Xi has acquired a long list of additional ones – so many that sinologist Geremie Barmé once quipped, using a term that others would later adopt, that we should call Xi China's "Chairman of Everything". One recently added title is "Commander-in-Chief". Neither of his immediate predecessors, Jiang Zemin and Hu Jintao, were called this – nor were Mao and Deng – but it flags an important thing about Xi: he's fond of presiding over massive parades of troops and weaponry. Commander-in-Chief is an interesting addition to the CoE's list of titles, but it's the two he got earliest that matter most, and each goes with a distinctive persona. There is a head-of-the-country "Statesman Xi" and a head-of-the-party "Chairman Xi".

Statesman Xi is a scholarly sort, who enjoys pondering texts by classical Chinese

TOMAS

He seems nothing like the crude "my-way-or-the-highway" patriarchal populists whose nationalist tirades come booming out of Manila, Moscow and Mar-a-Lago

Xi peppers his speeches with nods to literature but likes to be filmed on battleships and sometimes speaks in martial tones

→ philosophers and the writings of Marx and Engels. He's sometimes joined on international jaunts by Peng Liyuan, his stylish wife, who impressed many with a speech she gave in English at the UN. They are the proud parents of a Harvard-educated daughter. Cosmopolitan, calm and cautious, Statesman Xi chooses his words with care and speaks the language of win-win globalisation. He seems nothing like the crude "my-way-or-the-highway" patriarchal populists whose nationalist tirades come booming out of Manila, Moscow and Mar-a-Lago.

Statesman Xi also seems to have little in common with Mao, the firebrand founder of the People's Republic of China. Mao loved to shake things up and pit classes against one another. Statesman Xi calls for social harmony and stability. These are things his predecessor, Hu, also emphasised. Mao lambasted Confucius as a patriarchal feudal figure. Statesman Xi venerates the sage.

Chairman Xi is a very different kind of

CHINA'S BOY CLUB

||||||||||||||||||||||||||||||||||||||||||||||||||

Xi Jinping: Chinese Communist Party General Secretary, 2012-
Hu Jintao: CCP General Secretary, 2002-2012
Jiang Zeming: CCP General Secretary, 1989-2002
Deng Xiaoping: varied titles, most powerful figure in the CCP and People's Republic of China, 1978-1997
Mao Zedong: varied titles, most powerful figure in the CCP and PRC, 1949-1976
Chiang Kai-shek: head of the National Party and the Republic of China (mainland 1928-1949, Taiwan 1949-1975)

individual from the person just described. This second Xi is a muscular nationalist who is a lot like members of today's global crop of strongman leaders. He is also like Chinese strongmen of the past, and calling him "Chairman Xi" brings one of these in particular to mind: Chairman Mao. There is logic to this. Mao was pitiless toward rivals, clung to power until death and was hailed as a great Marxist theorist. His face and a book of his sayings seemed to be everywhere in China half a century ago. After his death in 1976, the party moved to regularise patterns of succession and eschewed personality cults. Things seemed to have finally moved into an orderly new normal of 10-year cycles by the time we got to Jiang and Hu. Each had a clearly designated heir apparent and handed the baton over after holding power for a decade. Books of their speeches were not published until they stepped down. Their slogans were not treated as holy writ.

Chairman Xi is in many ways a throwback to Mao. He has had the constitution changed so that he can rule indefinitely rather than be limited to two five-year terms as head of state, as Jiang and Hu were. His words are invested with sacred meaning. His face and his books are ubiquitous. He is suspicious of creative work that does not serve the party, as Mao was, and is hostile to critical thinking.

Whereas Statesman Xi is eager to ease his country into the international order and make friends, Chairman Xi is determined to extend Beijing's reach. He does this indirectly (via international projects designed to make weaker countries dependent) and directly (via putting buildings, including military installations, on atolls that other countries claim are theirs). Chairman Xi is not interested in claiming just tiny islands in the South China Sea and tightening the screws on a bigger island in the Pearl River Delta (Hong Kong). He also makes statements that suggest he wants to be remembered as the taker of a much bigger island: Taiwan. Chairman Xi wants to Make China Great Again.

It may seem strange to use for Xi a phrase that brings US President Donald Trump to mind, as surely as the term "Chairman" conjures up Mao's ghost. Here again, though, there's a logic. Statesman Xi is nothing like Trump, but the same cannot be said of Chairman Xi. Like Trump, he has no tolerance for dissent and views critics as traitors. In spite of trade war tensions and White House criticism of China, Chairman Xi seems at times to be living Trump's dream. Trump's fantasy USA would be one in which people never saw newspaper stories or television broadcasts that criticised or mocked the leader. Chairman Xi's actual China is one in which the Great Firewall keeps negative coverage of Xi hidden.

It's easy to list things that make the composite Xi both like and unlike Trump, Russian President Vladimir Putin and President Rodrigo Duterte of the Philippines, as well as both like and unlike Mao and Hu. He also has things in common with, but is in some ways different from, China's pre-1912 emperors. And he is in some ways most like, though also in some ways quite unlike, Chiang Kai-shek, the Nationalist Party leader who was Mao's great rival – sometimes called "President" and sometimes "Generalissimo". Chiang, like Xi, had a stylish wife who impressed Americans with an English language speech (in her case before Congress) and celebrated Confucian values. He was, like Xi, a muscular nationalist with little patience for dissent. But Chiang despised Marx, while Xi claims his theories are just an improved form of Marxism. In Chiang's time, China was weak; in Xi's time, it is strong.

One thing we can say about Xi is that he is definitely a strongman leader, even if he does not go in for the crude displays of machismo that figures such as Putin engage in. There are, however, more urbane sorts of tough autocrats. Hungary's prime minister, Viktor Orbán – the college activist and law student turned die-hard enemy of the Central European University – comes to mind. One can be both an intellectual of sorts and intensely anti-intellectual.

And it's worth keeping in mind the way Kam Louie, a leading theorist of Chinese gender, treats machismo in China, linking it to *wen* and *wu* strands of masculinity. *Wen* traits are associated with "cultural attainment"; *wu* ones with "martial valour". Mao, despite his

TESTING LOYALTIES

Chinese journalists must now pass a mandatory exam that tests their loyalty to President Xi Jinping, according to a notice from China's media regulator that was recently sent to many state-owned news organisations across the country. The government-designed app will test knowledge of "Xi Jinping Thought". It is made up of five parts, including a section on Xi's "important thoughts on propaganda". Journalists must answer 80 out of 100 questions correctly. Those who fail will not be issued a press pass. The test can only be retaken once; failing twice would effectively end a journalist's career. Journalists have said they are not sure if they would have to take the test each time they renew their press cards, which happens every five to six years.

tirades against the intelligentsia, prided himself on writing poetry to show his *wen* side, and he boasted of his battlefield accomplishments to show his *wu* side. Similarly, Xi peppers his speeches with nods to literature but likes to be filmed on battleships and sometimes speaks in martial tones, as he recently did in Delhi, about those who try to divide China being certain to be "crushed".

How well the strongman label fits Xi showed through in a private speech, which was later leaked, in early 2013. In it, he expressed a view of the final leader of the Soviet Union with which Orbán and Putin would likely agree. He claimed that Moscow's communists lost an empire and allowed their country to spiral downwards because no one there was "man enough" to deal firmly with the situation. There may be no one person Xi is entirely like, but he has made it clear that there is one person he is determined to not be like. This man, who many in the West admire for his flexibility but Xi views as a weakling to be despised, is former Soviet leader Mikhail Gorbachev. ✖

Jeffrey Wasserstrom is chancellor's professor of history at the University of California, Irvine, and the author of Vigil: Hong Kong on the Brink, which is set to be published in February 2020

Challenging Orbán's echo chamber

Budapest's new mayor has signalled that he wants to speak out for those that Viktor Orbán has tried to silence, reports **Viktória Serdült**

48(04): 12/14 | DOI: 10.1177/0306422019895700

"**B**UDAPEST BELONGS TO everybody: to right and left, to greens and liberals. Those supporting the government and those who do not. Rich and poor, young and old, women and men, singles and families."

So said Gergely Karácsony in his October inauguration speech as mayor of Hungary's capital city. These sentiments might seem unremarkable, but they come against a backdrop of conservative "family" policies promoted by the government.

Just a month earlier, a peculiar photo started circulating on social media: eight middle-aged men in suits sitting in the front row of a conference held in Budapest. What made the photo unusual was not the line of high-ranking politicians and church dignitaries in itself, but the fact that the Budapest Demographic Summit was focused on raising fertility rates in the region.

The event was far from the dystopia of The Handmaid's Tale as there were plenty of women in attendance, even as speakers. Yet the solutions offered for fighting low birth rates were perfect examples of the populist government's approach to the "obligations" of its citizens.

"Having children is a public matter, not a private one. It's not an individual obligation but a social and demographic necessity," said László Kövér, speaker of the Hungarian parliament, adding that childless people were "not normal" and "stand on the side of

death". Meanwhile, Miklós Kásler (the minister responsible for family policies) has emphasised the need for returning to Christian values. "Women will give birth if they want to, if they feel the urge, if they are raised to do so," he said.

Right now, government policies are pushing a particular set of values and in doing so leaving those that do not conform feeling like outsiders. For instance, women who bear four children are exempted from personal income tax for life. There is a cash incentive for large families to buy seven-seat vehicles. Families are entitled to loans of more than $30,000 that are written off if they have three children.

But couples must be married to qualify for the loans, and families who fail to produce the required number of children will have to pay the interest and the loans back, a provision that puts pressure on new mothers.

"My first child was conceived three months after we decided to have a baby. The second one took years because my husband worked abroad and I had health issues. I am already 39 and afraid of what will happen if we are not able to have a third one," said one mother, Viktória.

Although religion does not play an important role in society and only 9% of Hungarians attend church services each week, Prime Minister Viktor Orbán likes to emphasise the importance of Christian values, such as marriage and family. He sees big families as tools for fighting migration. If Hungarian women can populate the country then there will be "no need to bring in foreign workers and Christian society will be protected from newcomers". He has even come up with a term for the system he wishes to build – he calls it Christian democracy, which in his view would elevate the nation above the individualism of liberal states.

Critics say the notion is a mixture of macho and populist nationalism which means those who do not conform feel squeezed out. The

RIGHT: An advert for Coca-Cola promoting LGBT acceptance. An MP in Orbán's party Fidesz took a homophobic stance against it, calling for a boycott of Coca-Cola products

rhetoric puts particular pressure on women (see p.72), who may feel reduced to being simply child-bearers while men defend the country against threats. Abortion is legal and available in Hungary, but it is far from easy to obtain to ensure a low take-up rate.

Discussions about gender are also considered a threat by Orbán. It has resulted in a ban on gender-study programmes at universities, and the government refuses to ratify the Istanbul Convention on violence against women.

"People are born either male or female, and we do not consider it acceptable for us to talk about socially-constructed genders rather than biological sexes," the prime minister's spokesman said.

> *"I am already 39 and afraid of what will happen if we are not able to have a third one," said one mother, Viktória*

The country – alongside Greece – came last in the EU's 2019 Gender Equality Index. Hungarian women are frowned upon if they want to pursue a career and are not satisfied with solely being mothers.

When Orbán was asked in 2015 why there were no women in his cabinet, he replied that "few women could deal with the stress of politics".

On the anniversary of the 1956 revolution, a group of protesters tore down the rainbow flag from a community centre and set it on fire

→ Anna Júlia Donáth, a Member of the European Parliament from opposition party Momentum, said: "The pro-government media portray politics as something that is for men in suits. They believe women should stay home and take care of the children." She also admitted that criticism sometimes made her doubt whether she was good enough for office.

But there is another angle to gender policies in Hungary.

"Contrary to most countries where grassroots or religious organisations have mobilised against the term 'gender', in Hungary it is the government that maintains the perception of danger, so that it can present itself as the protector of the country," said political scientist Eszter Kováts.

When it comes to LGBT groups, the government is also making its views clear. The country's constitution states that marriage is possible only between a man and a woman, thereby making it difficult to change the legal recognition of gay and lesbian relationships from registered partnerships to marriages. LGBT people are not allowed to adopt, are not allowed access to artificial reproductive techniques and cannot take each other's names.

According to an EU survey, more Hungarians would be content with a Roma prime minister than with a homosexual one. (Roma are another group regularly demonised in the country.)

Anti-gay sentiment is also fuelled by state rhetoric. Recently, a Fidesz MP called for a boycott of Coca-Cola after its advertisements featured a gay couple, and the speaker of parliament, Kövér, often makes homophobic comments. "Morally there is no difference between the behaviour of a paedophile and the behaviour of someone who demands such things," he said, referring to marriage and adoption rights for gay people.

These public comments have also emboldened far-right groups. On the anniversary of the 1956 revolution, a group of protesters tore down the rainbow flag from a community centre and set it on fire. The police were nowhere to be seen.

LGBT people increasingly feel the burden when trying to reach out to wider society. Getting to Know LGBT is a school programme that was launched by the Labrisz Lesbian Association in November 2000. Its sessions are run by trained volunteers who help students understand the concept of LGBT rights and answer any questions. Last year, the programme was attacked by MP Dóra Dúró, who called it "homosexual propaganda".

"We get fewer invitations to schools, because some principals are afraid of what people and the government would say," said an activist.

Views of homosexuality differ depending on location: in the countryside, it is not only LGBT people themselves who face obstacles but their families and supporters of gay rights as well. Homosexual people from smaller towns and villages often move to Budapest, not only for jobs but also because they don't want their families to be stigmatised, and the capital is generally more accepting. A young couple speaking to news website Abcúg recently complained that, in the countryside, being gay was a bigger disadvantage to them than being Roma.

But among the calls for traditional values, the government rhetoric has had another impact: more people are fighting back. Karácsony, the new mayor, has already vowed to stand up for the rights of LGBT people, religious minorities and the homeless. And if he keeps to those promises, next year the rainbow flag will be flying above the city hall during Budapest Pride.

It might be a small gesture but it's a huge statement. ⊗

Viktória Serdült is a Hungarian journalist and works for hvg.hu, one of the few independent news sites in Hungary

Taking on the lion

Stefano Pozzebon reports from Brazil on the journalists who are standing up to the presidential onslaught

48(04): 15/17 | DOI: 10.1177/0306422019895712

BRAZILIAN PRESIDENT JAIR Bolsonaro recently posted a clip on Twitter comparing himself to a majestic lion surrounded by hungry hyenas. In his rhetoric, the hyenas are all those that this strongman labels as the enemy of the people – for example, the supreme court, opposition parties, his own party members and, often, the media.

He later removed the video and apologised for it, but his apology clearly lacked weight. Another similar video emerged, while he was in Saudi Arabia in October. This 20 minute clip on Facebook saw him attacking the media as "putrid" and "immoral" after a story emerged in October connecting him to the murder of a human rights activist in Rio de Janeiro.

These are clear reflections of how the former army captain sees himself, and his relationship with others. Bolsonaro's relationship with journalists is nothing short of confrontational: he didn't take part in pre-election debates, he regularly slams media companies and he often uses his personal social media channels to criticise or make fun of reporters.

This can all leave journalists feeling at risk. Patrícia Campos Mello never previously felt the need to use security personnel, even when reporting in conflict areas, such as the Turkish-Syrian border, or Ebola-plagued Sierra Leone.

But her newspaper, Folha de São Paulo, had to employ a bodyguard for three weeks last year to protect her in her home town after receiving threats from Bolsonaro supporters.

"It was very weird," Campos Mello said. "I've never had a bodyguard because I think it's intrinsically against being a journalist: you have to be in the same position as everybody else. So it was very strange that I needed a bodyguard in Brazil just because of some stories I had worked on."

Campos Mello's phone number was passed on to WhatsApp groups of Bolsonaristas who started attacking her, showing up at events where she was scheduled to take part and name-calling her on the street. After receiving personal threats and threats against her family, she decided to cancel all public engagements for a month, and the newspaper's parent company hired security on her behalf.

Even though the threats have stopped, she says she is still regularly confronted at political rallies and events.

Campos Mello is clear about the involvement of Bolsonaro in this dangerous game. She says it normally starts with a meme that attacks the journalist, often showing his or her face and some personal detail. The meme is tweeted to one of Bolsonaro's accounts.

"Then the president retweets it, and the president has over five million followers, →

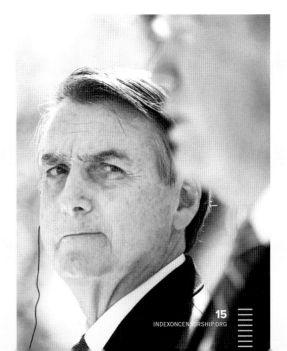

RIGHT: President Jair Bolsonaro with US President Donald Trump at a press conference at The White House, Washington DC, in March 2019

→ so once he retweets it you have all those followers and bots going after you," she said.

"And what usually happens is that they have your phone number and start calling you at all hours and throw insults at you."

This role of Bolsonaro marshalling his troops online is highlighted by other members of the media. Journalists point out that these attacks are often directed at women with the intent of scaring and silencing them, focusing on their physical appearance rather than their record.

Ana Freitas, a journalist who worked as a political reporter for several years before joining the fact-checking start-up Aos Fatos, agrees that the president's online behaviour has deep consequences for Brazilian society. "I think [Bolsonaro's] personal opinions kind of authorise opinions that people in the past were ashamed of sharing, and not only against women but also against homosexuals and other groups."

For many of Bolsonaro's supporters, his strong personal views and comments – such as when he appeared to enjoy a meme comparing French first lady Brigitte Macron unfavourably with his own wife – are simply part of the president's online persona and should not be confused with his political record.

I've never had a bodyguard because I think it's intrinsically against being a journalist: you have to be in the same position as everybody else

This is part of a wider debate taking place around the world, in countries such as India under the government of Narendra Modi, Turkey under Recep Tayyip Erdogan and the USA in the Donald Trump era. Many of these leaders enjoy a direct relationship with their political base and often this relationship is fuelled by attacks against their opponents and critics, with the media being one of the favourite targets. The base often applauds because it portrays the politician as an "authentic" character, as opposed to the camera-friendly, constructed persona of many contemporary politicians.

But media advocates worldwide agree that this resurgent "macho culture" from politicians is directly harming freedom of the press, and the health of democracy with it. According to the 2019 Freedom and the Media report by Freedom House, "in some of the most influential democracies in the world, populist leaders have overseen concerted attempts to throttle the independence of the media sector". Attacks against the press are often the precursor to further reductions in civil liberties and personal rights. Such is the current state in Brazil, which is a country that still enjoys a healthy democratic debate but where the media feel under attack.

Campos Mello said: "If you compare [Brazil] with Venezuela or Nicaragua, we may even feel bad about complaining because we are not getting arrested or anything. But compared with what used to be the environment for media in Brazil, I think now there's a striking difference."

She points at potential legislation being discussed that could hamper the finances of media groups at a time when the government has already limited public advertisements and notices in newspapers. A damaged outlet could find it more difficult to publish critical pieces that could result in lawsuits and litigation. Campos Mello's newspaper is one of the most trusted outlets in the country and has fought, and won, several defamation cases in the past 12 months, but smaller players might not be able to afford to instruct a similar team of lawyers.

The government also has influence on these defamation trials. Campos Mello was sued by Bolsonaro over an article she wrote in 2018. The trial took place in September 2019 and was won by Folha, but Campos Mello says the court allowed only Bolsonaro's witnesses to testify, and declined to hear any defence witnesses, including Campos Mello herself. "That's when I think it's scary, when they start to gain a lot of control over the judiciary system … and then I think we are walking towards a Poland scenario or a Hungary scenario," she said.

Personal attacks against reporters, financial restrictions and defamation suits are just some of the weapons Brazil's powerful people employ against the media. Another strategy is simply making journalists' jobs more difficult. Until this year, any statement by the president was posted online, but recently many of the smaller pronouncements or interviews have not been published.

"We used to have everything in the same place and [it was] easy to find, and now we have to scroll through YouTube and television channels to verify what the president said and when. It's a small thing, but it makes the journalist's job much harder," said Freitas, from Aos Fatos. This media start-up was founded in Rio de Janeiro in 2015 as a service to verify politicians' statements and separate facts from fake news. It rose to prominence during the 2018 election, when false information was being spread on social media with no control whatsoever.

"One example from last year was this story about the voting machines being controlled to favour the Workers' Party candidate," said Freitas. "It was completely false, but before we were able to prove it, the story was shared more than 700,000 times on social media."

Aos Fatos launched a new project this year to check every statement made by the president. In the first nine months of the year, it found Bolsonaro had released more than 385 false or incorrect statements. Its prominence came at a cost: its website is under constant attack from hackers trying to infiltrate the server and shut down the site. The company now employs a coder whose sole role is to repel these attacks.

But amid increasing challenges, Brazil is witnessing a flourishing of new digital-first outlets, more adapt at surviving the changing environment. Aos Fatos, founded by a team of former political reporters, is just one of them.

It portrays the politician as an "authentic" character, as opposed to the camera-friendly, constructed persona of many contemporary politicians

Many others, such as Midia Ninja, Agência Pública and Marco Zero, are trying to establish themselves as independent outlets, relying on donations by foundations and crowdfunding campaigns rather than the usual mix of advertisements and public funding that sustains much of the Brazilian media.

An outlet that has gained particular prominence this year is the Manaus-based news agency Amazônia Real, which specialises in environmental and indigenous coverage. It was founded in 2013 by two reporters, Elaize Farias and Kátia Brasil, who used to work in the traditional media until they found themselves out of jobs after a round of newsroom cuts.

Thanks to an initial grant by the Ford Foundation, the pair managed to fund Amazônia Real and find a niche in quality reporting on the Amazon. Bolsonaro's election, while presenting them with the same challenges that other outlets face, is giving new prominence to the region.

"The same day that Bolsonaro got elected, two attacks against indigenous territories took place," said Brasil. "That was the start."

The 2019 deforestation fires also increased the news agency's visibility, and Amazônia Real now receives visits from more than 180 countries, totalling an average of more than 60,000 unique readers per month. The success of the agency, Brasil says, is a testament to journalists' commitment.

"It's our duty. If we didn't have the guts to do this job, we would be silenced and, right now, we simply cannot allow being silenced." ⊛

Stefano Pozzebon *is a journalist based in Caracas, Venezuela. He regularly reports from Brazil*

Seven tips for crushing free speech in the 21st century

Rob Sears presents the ultimate "censorship how-to" for the modern strongman

48(04): 18/19 I DOI: 10.1177/0306422019895714

SO YOU'VE SEIZED control of your nation (hurray!) and now you're trying to stifle dissent. Simple, right? Not in the age of the internet. For the modern strongman, kicking down doors is no longer enough. To really shut up your enemies these days, you'll need to master a raft of sophisticated techniques, leaving kicking down doors as something you do just as a hobby, like whittling wooden spoons or brewing your own beer.

But tricky as the art of contemporary censorship may seem, plenty of modern despots with no apparent technical inclination are doing it brilliantly – and with this how-to guide, you can, too. It may seem complicated at first, but remember: you're a strongman. You've got this.

Tip #1: Take an evening course

The internet has been called history's greatest democratising force, so obviously you'll want to get on top of that. But how? Fortunately, training seminars are available, courtesy of China's President Xi Jinping, the original

digital authoritarian. He's already put on events to help 50 countries including Saudi Arabia, Thailand and Libya crack down online. So throw a few tonnes of rare earth minerals or a big arms contract his way and you, too, could soon be learning how to set up your very own version of the Great Firewall (the vast security and surveillance apparatus that governs online life in China).

Tip #2: Don't be afraid to ask for technical help

DNS interception… packet filtering… URL blocking… this could be an IT nightmare, and you've got a feeling your generals are only pretending to understand the jargon. Luckily, plenty of companies are happy to give technical support in exchange for a little of the national wealth you've looted. Canadian company Netsweeper, for example, creates the software used by Kuwait, UAE, Yemen and others to filter news and political opinion and block LGBT content. The company points out it takes no responsibility for how its products are used – but that's fine. Neither will you.

Tip #3: Assemble a world-class troll army

A record-setting Olympic squad and elite personal guard are all very well, but the ultimate strongman status symbol these days is a platoon of trolls. They may not look like much at your birthday parade but just wait until you put them to work. Maybe you'd like to prank other countries' electorates in the mode of Russia's Vladimir Putin, or flood your domestic audience with WhatsApp propaganda like India's Narendra Modi. Either way, a shit-posting special unit is this decade's despot must-have.

Tip #4: Quietly buy up your critics

Owning the media channels in your country is Despotting 101, but with innovative new corporate structures, an even more cunning move is available: doing it in secret. Earlier this decade, mysterious front companies bought up leading Venezuelan news providers Ultimas Noticias and El Universal. Even now it's not 100% clear who was behind the purchases but, conveniently for President Nicolas Maduro, the papers quickly moved to a markedly more pro-government line. The most challenging thing about pulling off such a manoeuvre? As someone used to slapping your portrait on every available surface, you'll have to resist the urge to take credit for once.

Tip #5: Let foreign companies do the hard work

You can't police everything that happens online, but don't worry. Gentle but consistent pressure is often enough to get overseas platforms to take up the slack on your behalf. As usual, China's Xi makes it look easy. Witness how, during the Hong Kong protests, Blizzard Entertainment ejected a popular video-gamer who voiced his support for the protesters, while Apple removed the Quartz news app for its coverage of the unrest – all without the Chinese authorities seeming to have to lift a finger. If you want to get a company to cravenly abandon its corporate values at your behest, just let the head honchos know you've been thinking of withdrawing their market access. Then let self-interest do the rest.

Tip #6: Focus your fire on the true enemy – journalists

When you're fighting trade wars and terrorists, it's important to remember who your real enemy is: any journalist who tries to question you. Take a leaf from US President Donald Trump's book and never miss an opportunity to address the reporters at your next five-hour press conference as "fake news", "the enemy of the American people" or the "lamestream media". After all, if you can successfully delegitimise the entire profession, no one will believe them when it comes to your various impeachable offences.

Tip #7: Don't forget about traditional media

With so many new formats to gag, it's easy to forget about books – those conveniently flammable things still found in the classrooms and libraries of most nations. Don't. Controlling textbooks is still a key part of the 21st century strongman's repertoire, enabling leaders like Recep Tayyip Erdogan of Turkey to trash evolution, deny genocide and strengthen his chokehold on the country. This summer, his forces seized and destroyed more than 300,000 books. So if you think a traditional book-burning could work for your administration, go for it! Just don't forget to torch the Kindle versions as well.

No one ever said being a modern strongman would be easy. But who knows? Once you've tried a few of these tips in the nation over which you preside, you might conclude we're living through a secret golden age of censorship and suppression, after all. ⊗

Rob Sears is author of The Beautiful Poetry of Donald Trump, Vladimir Putin: Life Coach and Choose Your Own Apocalypse with Kim Jong-un & Friends

"Media must come together"

Journalists need to stand up and shout about why media freedom matters, New York Times lawyer **David E. McCraw** tells **Rachael Jolley**

48(04): 20/23 I DOI: 10.1177/0306422019895715

WORRIED ABOUT AUTHORITARIAN global leaders putting the media under pressure to stop covering stories? You are not alone.

David E. McCraw, the New York Times deputy general counsel, is all over this subject – and not only because he knows what it feels like when the leader of your country starts trying to call out the work you do as traitorous.

This is a favourite tactic of authoritarians the world over, not just US President Donald Trump.

McCraw has worked on freedom of expression projects in Kuwait, Russia, Yemen, Montenegro and Bahrain, so he knows what the risks are for the whole world when the US president starts slowly spelling out his contempt for the media.

In the nearly two years since he started writing his book, Truth in Our Times: Inside the Fight for Press Freedom in the Age of Alternative Facts, the lawyer has seen the world slide further down a precipice where leaders of countries tip further and further in their contempt for journalists.

McCraw said: "[When] I began writing this book in the very early parts of 2018, I was seeing how much authoritarian governments were mimicking the language that we were hearing from the Trump administration."

And he is aware things have become considerably worse. "It did not seem as compelling at that moment as it does now," he said.

"The pushback against press freedom around the world has gained new life over the course of the past two years."

His career is high level and impressive. He is at the forefront of dealing with freedom of information litigation (he sued President Barack Obama's administration more than 25 times for withholding information and forced the disclosure of secret documents on a range of topics including CIA drone strikes in Yemen) and heads up the New York Times crisis response when its journalists get kidnapped.

In October 2016, a letter McCraw wrote to Trump's lawyer defending the paper's right to publish a story about two women who claimed to have been groped by Trump became one of the lasting artefacts of the presidential campaign. The letter was viewed and shared by millions of readers as it went viral in the heat of the presidential race.

He describes these times as "disquieting" and feels it is time for the media to come together.

"The physical violence against journalists, interfering physically with their ability to cover stories, all of those things have now become a much greater problem," he said.

While he was writing the book, a gunman attacked the Capital Gazette newspaper in Maryland, killing five people, yet the White House press secretary declined to say that the press was not the enemy of the people.

What have been the other symbols of a dark period for media freedom?

"We were truly astonished with President Trump standing with [Brazil's President Jair] Bolsonaro and applauding him for using the term 'fake news' on the steps of The White House. For me that was a very dark moment for press freedom worldwide."

Where once the rest of the world might have worried about the implications for their foreign policy and negotiations with the USA if they started locking up their journalists, it is clear that, following the indications from the Trump White House, this is not an issue anymore. The gloves are off everywhere.

And when macho leaders flex their muscles against the media they often do so with the aim of taking the public with them.

McCraw worries about a Hill-Harris poll

in 2019 that showed 33% of US citizens believed that the press was the "enemy of the people", and an earlier Ipsos Mori poll that found that 26% thought the president should have the power to close down news organisations if they misbehaved.

He said: "The idea that a quarter of US citizens feel that the president should have the power to punish the press is chilling. Rather than talk about how we can make press organisations better, they feel the press has failed them – they are endorsing the idea of the president using some kind of authoritarian measure to shut them down.

"Elections sometimes come up with very, very bad results and courts make silly decisions, but our response is not 'let's stop having elections' or 'stop having courts' – our response to that is to make institutions stronger."

But McCraw, whose CV also includes teaching at Harvard Law School, believes that the media as a whole can do more to combat some of those verbal zingers being sent their way. "We in the press have more power than we think to change those numbers."

He believes this has begun by talking about the value of press freedom and taking it out of partisan camps. "The discussion in the US has been too much centred on the idea that press freedom is something that the left wants and the right is against – that is a false dichotomy."

The press, whatever its politics, needs to be able to speak out for media freedom and its

> *The seeds of this campaign were planted right here, in a country that has long prided itself on being the fiercest defender of free expression*

place in a democracy, he adds.

"We are competitors. There is no question that the NYT is a competitor to the Wall Street Journal, to other publishers and broadcasters, but there are times when we have a common interest and we should be willing to come together."

And then there's this idea being pushed by those in power that wish the public to distrust the news and that the media is one big elite that never moves out of New York City. Again, this is when talking more about

ABOVE: The Boston Globe references their editorial defence of press freedom and a rebuke of President Donald Trump

The idea that a quarter of US citizens feel that the president should have the power to punish the press is chilling

→ how journalism works – and who does the work – can be helpful.

He says that the NYT recently published the home towns of everybody covering the presidential campaign on its behalf to show that its reporters hailed from everywhere.

"It showed that these were not people that had grown up clustered together in an ultra-liberal precinct on the Upper East Side of Manhattan: they were from all over the country, they came with different backgrounds.

"That's a very small step to help our readers understand that we represent America. You may not like what we do sometimes, but we are part of the fabric of the country."

He also feels that opening up some of the mystique of journalism brings the public closer.

"One thing we are seeing is simply greater transparency about how journalism gets done," he said. "I do think understanding that is important."

These things shed light on what is happening in newsrooms, but he says there are also shifts within news organisations themselves.

Where journalists and news media directors didn't previously see it as their job to speak up for the principles of freedom of speech and the media, the times are changing.

In September 2019, the NYT's publisher, AG Sulzberger, made a speech at Brown University, Rhode Island, on the importance of this. He spoke of how the NYT prepared its reporters for tough assignments, saying: "But we've long taken comfort in knowing that in addition to all our own preparations and all our own safeguards, there has always been another, critical safety net: the United States government, the world's greatest champion of the free press. Over the last few years, however, something has changed.

"Around the globe, a relentless campaign is targeting journalists because of the fundamental role they play in ensuring a free and informed society.

"And, perhaps most troubling, the seeds of this campaign were planted right here, in a country that has long prided itself on being the fiercest defender of free expression and a free press."

McCraw pointed out: "There was a time, I think, when people in Sulzberger's position did not want to look like they were adversaries against the president. We want to be seen as being honest brokers of information about the administration, but we have come to the point when that kind of silence and that kind of reticence is no longer fair or useful."

There is a risk for journalists in the USA and elsewhere, he believes, in not being willing to speak up about this vital element of freedom.

"The risk goes to the very heart of why we have supported free expression for so long – that is we become vulnerable to inequity, we become vulnerable to the worse sort of leadership, we become vulnerable to governments that are corrupt." ⊗

Rachael Jolley *is editor-in-chief of Index on Censorship*

David E. McCraw*'s Truth in Our Times: Inside the Fight for Press Freedom in the Age of Alternative Facts is published by St Martin's Press*

TRUMPED ON THE MACHO FRONT?

How does President Donald Trump measure up against former US heads of state when it comes to his macho man image? JAN FOX wields the measuring tape

"**TRUMP. FINALLY SOMEONE** with balls!" read the popular supporters' T-shirts worn at rallies. In his first term in office, US President Donald Trump has been photographed doing "manly" things such as hanging out with truck drivers and bikers.

His "tough guy" rhetoric includes praising Republican congressman Greg Gianforte when he body-slammed a reporter, saying: "He's my guy."

The president also claimed he would stop a school shooting "even if I didn't have a weapon". And when Isis leader Abu Bakr al-Baghdadi was killed in November, Trump commented that the USA did not ask the Russians about flying over their controlled area – they told them they were going in. Even his hair defies nature. This tough guy is in charge.

But then there's the perma-tan, the gold jewellery, the obsession with his appearance and, of course, hiding behind Twitter to insult his enemies rather than calling them out for a real duel. So just how macho is this man? How does the 45th president measure up on the machometer against his White House predecessors? And who else flexed their presidential muscles to threaten freedom of expression?

Theodore Roosevelt (26th president – 1901-09): "He was a classic case of macho. The real thing," said Mike Purdy, presidential historian and author of 101 Presidential Insults. "Like Trump, he had a huge ego but he led a strenuous life (after a sickly childhood). He was praised for his bravery at the battle of San Juan Hill (1898), went on safaris to Africa and up the Amazon and had a real toughness, but also did a lot of good." He was known for keeping wild animals at the White House, including a lion, giving his name to the teddy bear and coming up with the idea of National Parks. A tough guy with a heart, then.

John Adams (2nd president – 1797-1801): This intellectual was maybe not the traditional macho man but, according to Purdy, Adams was an "in your face guy – he said what he thought and made no bones about it. He also had a big ego".

He made one of the biggest transgressions against freedom of expression with the Alien and Sedition Acts of 1798, which limited freedom of speech generally, limited the press and was anti-immigrant. "This was a huge stain on the nation," said Purdy.

Andrew Jackson (7th president – 1829-37): Also perceived as a classic macho man, Jackson was feted for his military successes, but is less celebrated for his white supremacism. A slave owner, he also sent Native Americans on the Trail of Tears – a forced relocation of indigenous people. Trump keeps a portrait of Jackson in the Oval Office and is said to model himself on the seventh president.

Lyndon B. Johnson (36th president – 1963-69): Though not what we typically think of as macho, LBJ nonetheless exhibits some of the same traits as Trump in terms of language – uncouth – and actions, using his 6ft 3ins height to his advantage. "He was the master of intimidation, standing right next to someone, being in their face and leaning in to them," said Purdy. Trump has used his own pull-you-in handshake and the leaning technique on several occasions.

Abraham Lincoln (16th president – 1861-65), Ronald Reagan (40th – 1981-89) and George W. Bush (43rd – 2001-09): Lincoln, like Reagan and Bush, would go out to his ranch or cabin and do manly things such as chop timber. Trump is more likely to head to the golf course. Reagan took a bullet on national TV in 1981 and gained respect for his manly comeback. But log-splitter Lincoln did briefly suspend the writ of habeas corpus, a bit of a blot on his freedom of expression copybook – although it was during wartime, which might be considered a mitigating circumstance.

THE VERDICT

"Trump is a tough talker and likes to use profanity to try to be tough, but we associate macho with physical prowess and bravery and Trump doesn't have those. He's more of a bully than a macho man," said Purdy. "He wants to be macho – for example, he loves the military – but he's not. He got out of serving in the military by perhaps questionable methods, so he doesn't measure up in those terms.

"He hides behind Twitter to hit back because he's a bully but also somewhat of a coward."

Would Teddy Roosevelt have used Twitter? "Maybe, but he was comfortable going face-to-face with people, which Trump is not."

California-based anthropologist Derek Milne said: "A lot of macho is bravado, and Trump is right up there in my book. We have a gun-slinger history in America, so violence and patriarchy are part of American culture, which is why we are predisposed to macho leaders. It's framed like it's about safety – a threat to the USA from outside or from within – and Trump really plays that aspect up."

Who's the biggest threat to freedom of expression? For Purdy, it's a given: "I'd say Adams and Trump are neck-and-neck in attacking freedom of expression, but I think perhaps Trump is worse. He's called the press the enemy of the people. He's used the power of his office to squash officials from being able to testify even when there's a subpoena. He's very strategic with the way he uses the media, which is very dangerous for the core principles of democracy." ⊗

Jan Fox is contributing editor (USA) for Index

Tools of the real technos

Mark Frary discusses the ways in which technology is being used against us by the powerful and meets the RealDonaldDrumpf

48(04): 24/26 | DOI: 10.1177/0306422019895716

STRONG-ARM LEADERS HAVE long maintained an iron grip on freedom of speech, backed up if necessary by brute force. The anonymity afforded by the internet and the ability to spread information quickly and freely did have these leaders running scared but, unfortunately for dissidents and activists, the boot is back on the other foot and it's all thanks to the technology which had been such a boon for freedom of expression.

Here we explore the ways in which leaders such as Russian President Vladimir Putin are using technology for their own purposes.

Smartphone takeover

Following the death of Saudi Arabian journalist Jamal Khashoggi in October 2018, who was murdered at the Saudi consulate in Istanbul, Canada-based Saudi dissident Omar Abdulaziz launched a lawsuit against Israeli company NSO Group, claiming its software played a part. Abdulaziz, a confidant of Khashoggi, asked the Canadian courts to ban the company from selling its products to Saudi Arabia and to seek damages.

NSO Group's most infamous product is the spyware Pegasus, which works by sending innocuous-looking links. If users click on them, the spyware is installed on their devices. Missed calls via WhatsApp or push SMS messages have also been revealed as ways for it to be installed. A brochure shared by security researcher Claudio Guarnieri reveals that Pegasus can "remotely and covertly collect information about your target's relationships, location, phone calls, plans and activities – whenever and wherever they are", as well as enabling real-time call monitoring.

WhatsApp has since filed a lawsuit against NSO Group saying it had used its servers to infect target devices in several countries with malicious code. NSO Group disputes the claims.

Index has previously reported on the use of Pegasus in Mexico, following an investigation by Citizen Lab and the New York Times that revealed messages sent to Mexican journalists were laced with Pegasus spyware. It was dubbed by some papers at the time as the "Mexican Watergate" (Autumn 2017, 46.03, p.82-3).

WhatsApp misuse

While messaging tools such as WhatsApp have proven useful to activists because of the end-to-end encryption they provide, they can also be used in ways that the company did not intend, as the example of Pegasus shows.

Another instance of this was revealed in Freedom House's Freedom On The Net report 2019, which said that the victory of Jair Bolsonaro in Brazil's October 2018 presidential election was "a watershed moment for digital

According to the report, supporters of Bolsonaro "spread homophobic rumours, misleading news and doctored images on WhatsApp"

election interference in the country". According to the report, supporters of Bolsonaro "spread homophobic rumours, misleading news and doctored images on WhatsApp".

The Organisation of American States found that the messaging platform was being used to send bulk messages to multiple numbers through scraping software obtained online, and that automated messages were being shared with groups.

Local newspapers also reported that Bolsonaro was benefiting from a network of big businesses using undeclared funds to disseminate pro-Bolsonaro messages via WhatsApp. Bolsonaro denied the accusations, qualifying the bulk messaging as "voluntary support".

WhatsApp has proved particularly useful in Brazil as the app is not used for just private messaging. As a result of many mobile phone operators allowing unlimited WhatsApp access to subscribers, people who cannot afford an internet plan are able to turn it into a social media site of sorts, with people joining groups and connecting to others they have never met.

OAuth phishing

In March 2017, Canada's Citizen Lab uncovered a wide-ranging campaign against Egyptian NGOs, lawyers, journalists and activists following a tip-off from the Egyptian Initiative for Personal Rights. EIPR had begun receiving an increase in suspicious emails related to Case 173, a legal case brought by the Egyptian government against NGOs over issues of foreign funding. Analysing the emails, Citizen Lab realised that they employed a technique known as OAuth phishing.

OAuth is a perfectly legitimate way for internet users to grant websites and applications access to their information without handing over the password and is widely used by Facebook, Google and Twitter.

The attack works like this: you receive an email purporting to be from your email provider inviting you to update your security setting and the email looks legitimate so you click on the link to take you to your security settings. In some attack variants, an OAuth

STIFLING PARODY

THE 45TH PRESIDENT of the USA is known for his love of Twitter, so it comes as no surprise that Donald Trump's opponents have turned to the micro-blogging platform as well. Some have even gone as far as setting up parody accounts, which Twitter allows as long as the bio and account name reflect the fact that the user is not affiliated with the real person.

The account @RealDonaldDrumpf, referring to Potus's historical surname, has some 90,000 followers – far short of Trump's 66 million, but still impressive. The account is managed by writer Richard Hine.

"I started the account in 2013 when 'fake news' still meant the humorous kind, eg The Daily Show and The Onion," said Hine in an interview with Index.

The idea that you can actually parody Donald Trump's Twitter is an interesting one.

"There is nothing so outrageous or stupid that I can say in the voice of Donald Trump that someone on the internet will not believe is actually being said by Donald Trump," he said. "Many of my tweets are actually previews of future Trump tweets."

But the account has attracted the ire of its subject.

"He got into a feud with me when I exposed his ongoing racism and stupidity regarding the Central Park Five [five men who were wrongly jailed for the assault and rape of a jogger in New York]. This appears to be the first time a celebrity engaged in, and lost, an argument with his own parody account on Twitter. After that, he blocked me and I remain blocked to this day."

dialogue box labelled Secure Mail opens, and by clicking on your email address you unwittingly give a third party the ability to send, read and delete your emails.

Citizen Lab was not in a position to identify the sponsor of the campaign, but those targeted were largely those parties charged by the Egyptian government in Case 173.

In January 2019, a further investigation by Amnesty International revealed that several hundred prominent Egyptian human-rights defenders, media outlets and staff of civil society organisations had been targeted by OAuth phishing attacks and that these "likely originated from government-backed bodies". →

Troll factories

Where there's an opinion on the internet, there's an internet troll not too far behind, ready to attack. Trolls have been around ever since the earliest days of online conversation, but in the past few years trolling has become industrialised.

In "troll factories", employees are paid to post disinformation or add comments to news stories and social media posts that discredit the writer or offer a contrary view.

The best known of these is the Internet Research Agency in St Petersburg, allegedly funded by oligarch Yevgeny Prigozhin, a restaurateur known as "Putin's chef" and a close ally of the Russian leader. The activities of the Internet Research Agency were revealed by whistleblower Lyudmila Savchuk, who worked undercover at the company for two months in 2015.

"It was a regular part of the job to write posts in which you praised Putin," said Savchuk. During her time there, a regular task was to "spread negative publicity on Ukraine".

The organisation was also called out in Robert Mueller's report for interfering in the 2016 US presidential election.

Search censorship

For some young people in open democracies, if you can't search it then it doesn't exist. Usually this happens if the wi-fi goes down, but sometimes it is because even the mighty Google holds up its hands and says it cannot find anything relevant.

Yet in countries such as China, the reason you get zero results is often far more chilling.

In 2009, digital activist Jason Ng noticed that the internet was blocked during riots in Xinjiang province. It inspired him to build a computer script to see which search terms were routinely censored on microblogging platform Sina Weibo. He found that 500 terms, including "tank", the names of government officials and "hairy bacon", a reference to Mao's preserved body, could not be searched for. Even seemingly innocent terms such as "today" found themselves out of favour with China's internet censors as they became linked to commemorations of the Tiananmen Square massacre.

But it's not just China censoring its search functions. Foreign companies operating in the country have been accused of doing it too. Online image resource Shutterstock, for example, runs a keyword blacklist for any user with a mainland China IP address. A spokesman said that the company was "bound to local laws". ⊗

Mark Frary is a regular writer for Index. He wrote De/Cipher, a guide to cryptography

Modi and his angry men

The Indian prime minister likes to put on a tough show and this plays well with mobs who follow his war cry, writes **Somak Ghoshal**

48(04): 27/29 | DOI: 10.1177/0306422019895718

FROM PREENING ON reality TV with Bear Grylls to rubbish-collecting on a beach near Chennai in the south, Indian Prime Minister Narendra Modi has starred in diverse roles. He has bragged about his humble origins as a tea-seller's son and referred to himself as a *chowkidar* (doorman) of the nation. But as varied as these roles and descriptions might be, there's one constant – Modi always comes out great and all those who say otherwise are damned.

In October this year, Modi invited a delegation of 27 members of the European Parliament to visit Jammu and Kashmir. The idea was to show this hand-picked team of international observers – 22 of them belonged to right-wing parties in their home countries – that all was well in the northern state. When MEP Chris Davies of the UK's Liberal Democrats agreed to join only on condition that he be allowed to move around freely, "unaccompanied by military, police or security forces", his invitation was withdrawn. It was a typical example of Modi's "strongman leadership": nothing short of unquestioning fealty is good enough for his administration.

Of course, it is worse for those within India. Take Kashmiris, for example. On 5 August, Modi's government abrogated Article 370 of the Indian constitution, under which Kashmir had enjoyed special privileges including a degree of autonomy since 1954. The decision was announced in parliament by a minister, Amit Shah, who cited a presidential order that sealed the fate of Kashmiris overnight. At the time of writing, Kashmir is reeling under a government-imposed communications ban. Mobile phone services remain patchy while access to the internet is suspended. This is the quid pro quo that Modi's government offered as its "solution" to the long-standing conflict in Kashmir. The silencing of a population of more than 12 million and the detention of local leaders are the fallout of its smug arrogance.

Concern for internal security is the government's ostensible reason for prolonging the lockdown. But another motivation is Modi's distaste for hearing public opinion that challenges him and his government's actions. An iron-fist stance is one way to achieve this.

Aggressive crackdowns by ruling governments are not unknown in independent India. From 1975 to 1977, Indira Gandhi, the then prime minister, imposed a state of emergency across the nation, leading to severe curbs on press and personal freedoms. Yet even this period of censorship and systematic repression was more an aberration in India's otherwise robust democratic fabric.

Since Modi, of the Bharatiya Janata Party, was elected with an overwhelming majority in 2014, the scene has changed radically. Free speech is a poisoned chalice in India now, and the crushing of dissident voices is the new norm. But it's not just Modi and his officials who are policing speech – it's people from all walks of life, and they've become an indispensable tool in maintaining Modi's image. A typical example is the recent fiasco over an open letter by 49 Indian celebrities addressed to Modi, asking him →

While Modi may be celebrated within India by his burgeoning tribe of followers, for others his tenure has fostered a climate of fear and intimidation

ABOVE: Indian Prime Minister Narendra Modi waves to supporters at a parade in April 2019, flanked by security guards

to take stringent action against the growing number of mob lynchings since he assumed office. The plea – signed by intellectuals such as historian Ramachandra Guha and filmmaker Shyam Benegal – enraged Sudhir Kumar Ojha, a lawyer. Ojha filed a petition in court against the signatories, accusing them of tarnishing "the image of the country", undermining "the impressive performance of the prime minister" and "supporting secessionist tendencies". After more than 180 cultural personalities condemned the court order, the case was dropped, but not before a point had been made: "If you are not

with Modi, you are with anti-India forces."

While Modi may be celebrated within India by his burgeoning tribe of followers, for others his tenure has fostered a climate of fear and intimidation. More than 250 people have been lynched since the start of Modi's rule. Most of the victims are Muslims or belong to marginalised castes, largely targeted for eating beef. The BJP's Hindu nationalist agenda extols the cow as "holy mother". Bands of men who go by the name of *gau rakshaks* (self-styled protectors of cows) terrorise the vulnerable for alleged smuggling of cows or possession of beef. They're the strongmen following their strongman's vision.

Many of these hate crimes are fuelled by the spread of fake news on social media, especially WhatsApp, which is another weapon in Modi's armoury. The escalating volume of disinformation has led to the rise of dedicated fake-news busters but the cycle of violence and vendetta remains unabated.

In many instances Modi projects an image of being aloof to suffering, such as when in 2015 an irate mob barged into the home of a 52-year-old Muslim man in a village near Delhi, accused him of keeping beef in his refrigerator and killed him. Modi maintained a studied silence for days, even as citizens took to the streets in protest. In 2017, a 15-year-old Muslim boy was called a "cow-eater" by a crowd during an altercation over seats on a train, assaulted, then thrown off. Again, Modi waited for days before condemning the incident.

If silence is Modi's steadfast ally, so is a section of India's fourth estate. As business interests of corporate media get tied up with political goodwill, ethics are compromised with impunity. Modi's thundering warnings to Pakistan make for headlines and spin-offs on prime-time television but criticism of his shortcomings are met with intimidation, online trolling and threats. Modi's supporters are quick to label dissenters "anti-nationals" or seditionists.

It started in 2016 with a group of students at the Jawaharlal Nehru University in New Delhi being charged with sedition – a draconian legal legacy of the colonial era – for allegedly raising "anti-India" slogans at an event. "Anti-national" is now common parlance and has even entered the jargon of governance. The latest data released by the National Crime Records Bureau lists offences perpetrated by "anti-national elements" as a new category of crime, although it doesn't define the term.

In Modi's India, it's par for the course to be abused as a "Pakistani terrorist" for not demonstrating patriotic fervour approved by the majority

Modi's government also instituted a controversial rule mandating cinemas to play the national anthem before every screening (see Spring 2017, 46.01, p.66-68). Those who didn't stand up during the anthem failed in the eyes of any staunchly nationalist audience around them. Even those with disabilities were not spared. Although the decree was reversed last year, the attacks haven't ceased. In Modi's India, it's par for the course to be abused as a "Pakistani terrorist" for not demonstrating patriotic fervour approved by the majority.

Even facetious memes have landed people in trouble. Police travelled 250km to arrest a 19-year-old tailor for sharing an allegedly "offensive and morphed" image of Modi over WhatsApp, mocking his doomed mission of cleaning up "black money". Fans of Modi, whose love for the camera is well documented, evidently favour only one kind of image makeover: one that projects their strongman leader as an everyday superhero. Modi cleans up strategically placed rubbish from streets, takes selfies with his buddy Donald Trump and roars back at Pakistan's nuke threats. That's the image they like.

As India's economic performance dips, it remains to be seen if the armour of a strongman leader will continue to protect his fortunes in the months to follow. For now, it has only a mere dent. It will take the collective will of Indians and a strong political opposition to unseat him from power.

Somak Ghoshal *is a journalist based in Bangalore, India. He writes on current affairs, LGBTQ+ rights, arts and culture*

Global leaders smear their critics

In a special investigation into how authoritarian leaders are sharing tactics, **Caroline Lees** uncovers five shocking techniques being used to frighten or damage their critics

48(04): 30/32 I DOI: 10.1177/0306422019895719

TRAITOR, WHORE, TERRORIST, pervert, fraudster. In the 21st century, smears deployed by autocratic governments against their political opponents have become ever more common, powerful and damaging.

The new strategies of repression have at their heart the relentless exploitation of social media, often using state-funded troll armies to find and monitor anyone critical of the regime, its leader or its policies – and then to repeatedly belittle, bully and besmirch them.

"We have entered an environment that suggests that authoritarian regimes have placed a premium on adapting and migrating their techniques to the digital landscape... to undermine the credibility of activists and oppositionists," said Christopher Walker, of the Washington-based National Endowment for Democracy.

There is growing evidence of what could be termed "authoritarian best practices" spreading from one country to another. Russia's repressive crackdown on non-governmental organisations began in 2005 by Moscow labelling those organisations that received overseas funding as "foreign agents" – a term synonymous with "spy", "traitor" and "enemy of the state".

This tactic has since been widely copied, including by Hungary, Pakistan and China, which recently brought in strict new laws to control and restrict NGOs. Some of these tactics are also widespread in Latin America.

Russia's use of troll armies to carry out large-scale attacks on critics and disinformation campaigns to promote Moscow have also been copied by other leaders.

In Mexico, this technique has been used for years against journalists. In June 2015, Index reported on the army of automated bots which swept in to silence dissent when President Enrique Peña Nieto's official visit to London attracted online protests (Summer 2015, 44.02, p.127-29).

Walker said: "The speed and opacity that is associated with social media initiatives can offer well-resourced and purposeful authoritarian powers a privileged position to attack independent voices. In an era of globalisation, through the use of widespread technologies the ability to hound and intimidate activists now transcends national borders."

A report last year from Oxford University's Samantha Bradshaw and Philip Howard, Troops, Trolls and Troublemakers, a Global Inventory of Organised Social Media Manipulation, detailed the state funding of "cyber troops" in 28 countries, including Azerbaijan, North Korea, Iran, Turkey, Poland and Ecuador. It concluded that such methods were "a pervasive and global phenomenon" and a danger to democracy.

"When you say a lie a million times on social media, it is a fact. If you have no facts, you have no truth," said Maria Ressa, a Filipina journalist often criticised by the government of President Rodrigo Duterte.

Index on Censorship's research below shows that there are five regularly used categories of smears currently favoured by authoritarian regimes:

1. "Traitor"

Accusing an opponent of working for "foreign interests", or even spying, to undermine the state.

After initially censoring coverage of the pro-democracy demonstrations in Hong Kong, Chinese state media recently launched a series of personal attacks against leading protesters, accusing them of being traitors and of colluding with "Western agents".

In August this year, Jair Bolsonaro, Brazil's right-wing president, accused the head of the country's space research agency, Ricardo Galvao, of treachery, alleging that he "worked for foreign NGOs". Galvao was sacked after his agency reported a statistic Bolsonaro did not like - that deforestation had increased by 88% over the previous year.

In the USA, government officials have recently been accused of orchestrating a smear campaign against Alexander Vindman, a White House security adviser who gave evidence against President Donald Trump over the Ukraine inquiry. Pointing out that Vindman was born in Ukraine (he moved to the USA as a baby), Trump supporters posted that he must be a spy, with one former White House official tweeting: "Some people might call that espionage."

The "traitor" smear has also been deployed by Hungary's prime minister, Viktor Orbán, in particular against the Hungarian-born philanthropist, George Soros. Orbán has accused Soros – and NGOs funded by his organisation – of working for "foreign interests" to undermine Hungary's government.

2. "Slut", "bimbo", "whore"
Sexualising female opponents to degrade and humiliate them has been described by Nina Jankowicz, of the Wilson Centre in Washington, as "sexualised disinformation".

Jessikka Aro, a Finnish journalist who

V. Kazanevsky

exposed pro-Kremlin troll factories in 2014, became a victim of their activities herself and was subjected to years of harassment online. The attacks included false claims that she was a prostitute soliciting officials from the CIA and Nato, and threats to rape and kill her. In Ukraine, doctored nude images of former Ukrainian politician Svitlana Zalishchuk appeared online after she criticised Russia.

In the USA, two far-right conspiracy theorists known for perpetuating false sexual assault claims against Trump's political opponents recently held a press conference to accuse Elizabeth Warren, a Democrat presidential candidate, of an affair with a former marine 40 years her junior. Meanwhile, Democrat congresswoman Katie Hill resigned after nude photos of her were leaked and published in the media.

3. Terrorist
A label to create fear and undermine opponents.

Since 2013, the Turkish government has →

In Ukraine, doctored nude images of former Ukrainian politician Svitlana Zalishchuk appeared online after she criticised Russia

→ waged a campaign against cleric Fethullah Gülen, President Recep Tayyip Erdogan's political rival, by claiming he runs an "armed terrorist network" with links to the CIA. According to documents provided to the Robert Mueller 2016 US presidential election inquiry, a lobbying firm owned by former Trump national security adviser Michael Flynn was contracted to dig up damaging information about Gülen, who lives in self-imposed exile in the USA. In November 2016, Flynn authored a comment article in The Hill, describing Gülen as "a shady Islamic mullah" and "radical Islamist".

Ethiopia has invoked the country's anti-terrorism laws against critics numerous times. Five journalists who had been reporting on human rights violations are currently being held on terrorism charges, although no evidence has yet been brought against them.

4. "Tax evader"

For the past three years, Maria Ressa, founder of influential news site Rappler.com, has been attacked and criticised by the Philippines government in the media, online and in the courts. Ressa has been accused of trying to overthrow the government and being a foreign agent, and has been charged with 11 separate offences under the country's tax evasion, cyber-libel and anti-dummy laws. She has also been trolled on social media, with allegations that she has links to the CIA, among many other claims. Ressa believes the personal attacks against her are linked to reports by Rappler that more than 20,000 people had been killed in the government's war on drugs – a number four times higher than the official figure.

In 2011, the Chinese government arrested and imprisoned the activist and internationally-renowned artist Ai Weiwei for 81 days before charging him with tax irregularities. He claimed the charges were politically motivated.

5. "Pervert", "pornographer", "paedophile", "rapist"

This range of smears and insinuations has long been used as a propaganda tool.

Once these allegations are made via social media they can become permanently associated

When you say a lie a million times on social media, it is a fact. If you have no facts, you have no truth

with the name of the accused. They have been regularly used in Russia against government critics. In 1997, the historian Yuri Dmitriyev uncovered human remains in a forest in Russia's northern Karelia region which provided the first evidence of mass executions during Stalin's Great Terror in the 1930s. At first, local authorities acknowledged the discovery and erected memorials to the thousands believed to have been killed there. But in 2016, as the site and Dmitriyev gained international attention and President Vladimir Putin sought to rehabilitate Stalin's reputation, official attitudes changed. Within months, the 63-year old historian was charged with child pornography and imprisoned. The charges were dropped in 2018 due to a lack of evidence, but weeks later he was arrested again and charged with sexual assault. He is currently awaiting a second trial.

Dmitriyev's case is not unusual in Russia. In September this year, anonymous posters claiming that Andrey Rudomakha, an environmental activist and government critic, was a "paedophile" were posted around the city of Krasnodar. The posters included photographs of Rudomakha as well as his home address.

But those making such smears can be caught out. In Poland, deputy minister of justice Łukasz Piebiak resigned after recordings emerged of him planning a smear campaign to spread salacious rumours about the private lives of 20 senior judges who had opposed unpopular government judicial reforms. ⊗

Caroline Lees is a regular contributor to Index and a former Sunday Times Afghanistan correspondent

Sexism is president's power tool

President Rodrigo Duterte of the Philippines is using extreme threats and expletives against female journalists as a way to shut them up. **Miriam Grace Go** reports

48(04): 33/35 I DOI: 10.1177/0306422019895720

ON LATE NIGHTS when the young man of the house came home drunk, he had a way of shaming his wife for locking him out. He would reportedly shout expletives for the neighbours to hear which included comments about her private parts. That is one of the many anecdotes that Earl G Parreño told me he picked up in Davao City in the southern Philippines while working on his book Beyond Will & Power, which was published recently.

The young man in that story is now 74 and the most powerful man not just in his home city but in the country. Rodrigo Duterte is still drunk – this time with power. He still clearly subscribes to the idea that sexual remarks are a weapon to dominate the weak, and that demeaning comments about someone's body can unsettle an opponent who would otherwise have the upper hand.

By all indications, Duterte perceives journalists who poke at his questionable or controversial policies as enemies, so that weapon is trained on us as well.

Just this September, Duterte railed at my news organisation, Rappler, in a speech before provincial vice-governors. He complained about how we supposedly played up the allegation of a self-proclaimed whistleblower that his (Duterte's) family was connected to the illegal drugs trade.

"These Rappler people. I said, this is the last straw, 'You sons of a bitch, your — smell! I just can't say it, your underarm or your —'. Yes, I'm being rude towards them. 'You leave me with no recourse. You disrespect my person'," he said, stopping short of directly mentioning vaginas.

Months earlier, also in relation to media coverage of that discredited witness, Duterte called Ellen Tordesillas, president of the investigative journalism group Vera Files, "every inch a prostitute".

Between those two incidents Duterte signed the Safe Spaces Act, a law that punishes a wide range of sexual offences, including a number that he himself had publicly committed or confessed to. When journalists pointed out the irony to his spokesman, Salvador Panelo, he replied: "You assume that the president is vulgar. He never was vulgar. When he cracks jokes, it was intended to make people laugh, never to offend. Being vulgar is different. You women should know that. We have to distinguish between someone who is coarse and someone who is just trying to make you laugh."

Journalists – especially women – aren't laughing.

Duterte's first display of sexism as president-elect was towards a female TV reporter. In a press conference in Davao City in May 2016, he wolf-whistled at GMA7 reporter Mariz Umali while she was asking a question about his prospective appointees to the cabinet. In that same press conference, Rappler reporter Pia Ranada pointed out to Duterte that what he had just done to Umali went against the anti-sexual harassment ordinance the city $\rightarrow$

This misogynist president has unravelled since, saying in speeches that he kept an eye on Vice-President Leni Robredo's legs during cabinet meetings

→ council had passed, and he had signed, during his term as mayor. Duterte's response? He wolf-whistled at Ranada, too.

When our reporter persistently asked him about his violation of the local law, the president-elect said: "I don't like your question. Next question."

This misogynist president has unravelled since, saying in speeches that he kept an eye on Vice-President Leni Robredo's legs during cabinet meetings; that he would make Pope Francis watch a supposed sex video of Senator Leila de Lima to make him regret giving her a rosary; that, as commander-in-chief, he would take responsibility for soldiers if they could each rape three women; that soldiers should shoot women communist fighters in the vaginas because women are "useless without them"; that if he were the boyfriend of the pretty town mayor who was seeking his endorsement, he'd hold on to her panties until they snapped; and that he molested their maid when he was a teenager.

Last February, Duterte was angry with former senator Francisco Tatad, who wrote in a newspaper column about the president's alleged sickness. Duterte told the columnist that his virility would prove he wasn't ill. "You want to know if I'm still up to it? Do you have a wife? Lend her to me!" he said.

Journalists' protests can go only so far. Can we sue Duterte for his sexist words or actions towards us? He is immune from lawsuits while in power. Can we boycott him in our coverage? He's the president. Can we expect media owners to come to their employees' defence against the highest official of the land? The prevailing mindset in the industry is that intimidating remarks from officials "come with the territory".

And there lies the bigger danger that Duterte presents. He is the president. When he displays misogyny and gets away with it, men can be emboldened to follow his example and women might become accepting of how their dignity is lowered.

Theresa de Vela, gender studies expert at Miriam College, previously explained to Rappler the concept of "gender socialisation" and how Duterte, with the rape jokes that come to him so easily, had made an "extremely harmful" contribution to how Filipinos develop their expectations of and attitudes towards the sexes.

"Leaders play a role in our socialisation because they represent one of the social institutions that mould our society... When you have a president doing that, you're adding to, reinforcing that sexual script that says sexual violence is acceptable behaviour and is part of the male behaviour to be in society. It is manly. It's what makes you an attractive male," De Vela said.

Duterte's supporters prove that this point is true, spreading gender-based vitriol on social media against journalists and the president's critics.

Rappler's Ranada has been threatened with rape after consistently asking hard questions of the president. So has Inday Espina-Varona, Reporters Without Borders prize for independence winner, for her hard-hitting columns and social media posts, and so has former Reuters photo-journalist Ezra Acayan's family after he documented Duterte's bloody war on drugs. Vice Asia-Pacific editor Natashya Gutierrez was called an "attention-seeking whore" when she was a Rappler reporter. A non-political

The prevailing mindset in the industry is that intimidating remarks from officials 'come with the territory'

journalist I know who wrote just one column critical of a Duterte policy found a photo of her daughter online, posted liberally by the president's supporters, wishing the young girl to be raped and dead. Rappler CEO Maria Ressa has been insulted with comments that she isn't attractive enough to be raped.

In a talk at Rappler's headquarters in December 2017, the International Centre for Journalists' Julie Posetti said female journalists were indeed "more vulnerable to online harassment" than their male counterparts were.

Drawing from her study of journalists' security in the digital age, she said cyber harassment against women journalists was sexualised and focused on their physical appearance, sexual orientation and family members, among other things. The intention of the attackers was to intimidate these women into abandoning

investigations they were doing, or to destroy their credibility when they criticised public figures and institutions.

Duterte thinks the problem is with women and not with him. Last March – ironically (again), at an event honouring women law enforcement officers – he said: "*Puta* (Bitch), you know, you women, you are depriving me of my freedom of expression.... You criticise every sentence or word I say, but that is my freedom to express myself… I am doing this because I am trying to bring you to the limits of despair."

He can try, all right. But expect us – women, journalists – not to get tired of pushing back. ⊗

Miriam Grace Go is news editor at
Rappler, based in Manila

ABOVE: Journalists and supporters of Rappler, including CEO Maria Ressa (middle) protest a move to revoke their registration

Rowson

48(04): 36/37 | DOI: 10.1177/0306422019895721

MARTIN ROWSON
is a cartoonist for
The Guardian and
the author of various
books, including
The Communist
Manifesto (2018), a
graphic novel adap-
tion of the famous
19th century book

Sounds against silence

Resistance to Turkey's most powerful is coming from a surprising quarter: rap musicians.
Kaya Genç reports

48(04): 38/40 I DOI: 10.1177/0306422019895722

TURKEY'S ARCHETYPAL MACHO leaders almost always come with a modernising agenda, a profound dislike for dissent and a determination to get their way. From Abdülhamid, the last significant Ottoman sultan, to Mustafa Kemal Atatürk ("the Father of Turks" who founded the republic) and the current president, Recep Tayyip Erdogan, known to his supporters as the "Chief", these traits are typically used to solidify power and muzzle free speech.

For decades, Turkey's dissidents pushed back against machismo. Popular culture, humour and irony became their main tools in combating toxic masculinity. But in recent years, especially after a government crackdown on civil freedoms in 2017, an unexpected new wave of dissent has risen in the form of rap music.

Susamam (I Can't Be Silent Anymore), a collaboration featuring 18 rappers, was released in September this year. On YouTube it has been viewed more than 36 million times, making music history and turning rap into a vehicle to fight Turkish machismo.

The 15-minute song is a manifesto of sorts about Turkey's male-dominated social structure. It opens with Şanışer, the stage name of the 32-year-old rapper Sarp Palaur. Sporting a baseball cap, Şanışer walks among crowds in Istanbul while a mechanical background voice warns against superficialities that direct Turks' minds away from their real problems.

Images of belly-dancers and other touristic cliches fill the screen before Fuat Ergin, one of the leading rappers, takes their place.

With his camouflage jackets, cargo pants and hunky presence, Ergin doesn't look like a feminist. But male greed, he says, is destroying nature. In Susamam, Ergin stands on a tank to rap about industrial waste and its pollution in rural Anatolia. Another rapper, Ados, takes the mic from him and warns about the climate crisis and droughts threatening Turkey's rivers. Şanışer joins them to ask viewers to break their silence. These rappers share a concern to protect nature from powerful men.

Server Uraz sings from inside a prison cell. He admits to remaining silent for years while journalists were imprisoned. "Now I'm too afraid even to tweet," he says. Şanışer scorns him for caring about only "third-wave coffee shops" and "start-ups", proclaiming: "If you were taken unlawfully from your home tonight, you wouldn't find even one reporter to write your story. Because they're all in jail."

In this segment and others, rappers confront macho values head-on. They tackle other social ills, too: the education system, the injustices of courts and road rage on highways are subjects of their criticisms. One rapper drinks wine, singing his lines drunk on a pavement.

OPPOSTIE: Şanşier, stage name of rapper Sarp Palaur, who is featured on Susamam

Another screams his lyrics to the mountains. Their performances are less a song than an outcry. These tough-looking guys passionately self-scrutinise.

Deniz Tekin, the only female performer in Susamam, sings about women's rights, and lists some of the horrors Turkish women →

On YouTube it has been viewed more than 36 million times, making music history and turning rap into a vehicle to fight Turkish machismo

This is why it's no small feat that they've stopped being proud of their cocks even for a few minutes

→ experience: husbands throw acid at their wives' faces, brothers kill sisters and call their crimes "honour killings", and supervisors expel female students from dormitories for so-called "improprieties".

Tekin also mourns Turkish women killed in recent years by men in positions of power. Münevver Karabulut's body was dismembered by the son of a Turkish tycoon who later committed suicide in prison. Şule Çet fell to her death from her boss's office in the skyscraper he owned – her family say she was pushed. Emine Bulut's estranged husband, who was a security guard, used a blade to cut her throat in public, as their child watched her bleed to death.

"No man is allowed to raise a fist against women!" rap the duo Sehabe and Yeis Sensura. "Yes, they are male, but they aren't human!" The segment shows instances of male violence against women at home and on public transport. Security cameras regularly capture men abusing women – in March this year, the owner of an entertainment venue in Beşiktaş punched a female employee in the face. "You will stand up when I enter the room," he said in the CCTV footage before attacking her. "Are you even human? How does one even get to this point?" they wonder in the song.

Naim Dilmener, one of Turkey's leading music critics, told Index: "Şanışer and his friends voiced their dissent about Turkey's present state. In their fight against sexism, those rappers tried to show that the opposition was not dead in the water [and] that they were willing to raise their voice."

Although Dilmener approaches rap music's new role with caution, he considers its critique of machismo to be a step in the right direction. "Like our rockers, Turkey's rap musicians are famed for their sexism," he said. "References, wordplay and swearwords in their songs

always adore masculinity. This is why it's no small feat that they've stopped being proud of their cocks even for a few minutes. I think we need a pile of these gestures for anti-sexism to truly triumph. Of course, Susamam can't by itself erase machoism from Turkish culture. But symbolically it is a huge deal to see rappers raise their voice."

Pro-government Turkish newspaper Yeni Şafak said the rap song was produced by terror groups, and accused foreign media such as the BBC and Deutsche Welle of bringing this "discourse of marginal leftist groups" to an international audience. The government issued a warning: "Art shouldn't be the vessel of provocation and political manipulation."

Pro-government trolls have attacked the Susamam rappers on social media, and on 17 September a complaint was filed in an Istanbul court against the song's contributors. One of them, Defkhan, soon announced he was "leaving the project" because of the "political momentum the song has gained". He tweeted: "I like my friends who've contributed to this song; I just don't like politics." But other celebrities, including the actor Ahmet Mümtaz Taylan and the rock musician Harun Tekin, announced their support for the song.

In 2014, Bülent Arınç, one of the founders of the ruling Justice and Development Party, famously proclaimed that women shouldn't be allowed to laugh in public. In the half-decade that has followed, machismo has grown on social media but so has dissent. Tahribad-ı İsyan, perhaps Turkey's most exciting rapper duo, sing about "dinosaur politicians" and nepotism among men in their segment of Susamam. They also repeat a famous political mantra, once used by socialists and feminists but now appropriated by men who have just had enough of machismo: "Don't be silent; as long as you remain so you'll be arrested next." ⊗

Kaya Genç *is an Index on Censorship contributing editor, based in Istanbul. His new book,* The Lion and the Nightingale, A Journey Through Modern Turkey, *is out now*

Un-mentionables

Some of the world's most powerful countries are ruled by men who pride themselves on their macho images. But their egos are fragile, and here are some of the things you just can't mention. **Orna Herr** reports

48(04): 41/41 I DOI: 10.1177/0306422019895723

DOES KIM JONG-UN of North Korea own a plane capable of flying to the USA? Who knows? When a summit with US President Donald Trump was being arranged in 2018, this question was posed by several media outlets, only to be ignored. And it's not the first time questions concerning his mode of international transportation have remained unanswered. Plane, train, boat – it's anyone's guess really.

Size matters
Bigly. Yuge. Trump's adjectives of choice are all about size, so call his hands small at your peril. And when it comes to crowds… well, according to former White House spokesman Sean Spicer, Trump's 2017 inauguration was witnessed by more people than any other inauguration in history. Photographs tell a different story.

Sticks and stones won't break his bones...
Russia's President Vladimir Putin likes to show he's the big guy, through martial arts, appearing topless on a horse and other "manly" displays. But this manly man can't handle any insults – so much so that he signed a bill this year making insults against him punishable by fines that can be more than $4,500, with 15 days in jail for repeat offences. What's an insult? "Putin is a fag" and "fantastical fuckhead" have already fallen foul.

Bear-faced lies
Winnie the Pooh, who came into being in 1926, is one of the best-loved characters in the world. Not, however, for China's President Xi Jinping. Censors have banned the cuddly bear in the country following jokey comparisons between the bear and Xi.

Potty mouth
It is not only critics of his government that Turkish President Recep Tayyip Erdogan wants to silence, it is critics of his decor. In 2015, Erdogan threatened to sue the leader of the opposition, Kemal Kılıçdaroğlu, for saying he had gold-plated toilet seats in his mansion in Ankara. The accusation was made in the context of Kılıçdaroğlu's ongoing criticism of Erdogan's lavish lifestyle, but it seems the specific mention of his indulgent bathroom design choice was one toilet seat too far.

Daddy's girl?
Brazil's President Jair Bolsonaro, who routinely shows contempt for women, extends such contempt to his own child. "I have five children. Four are men, and then in a moment of weakness the fifth came out a girl," he said. Best not mention his daughter, then.

Orna Herr is the editorial assistant at Index

CREDIT: CSA-Archive/iStock

Salvini exploits "lack of trust" in Italian media

Matteo Salvini stirs up public distrust in Italy's media. But part of the problem is many Italians did not trust journalists in the first place, writes **Alessio Perrone**

48(04): 42/44 | DOI: 10.1177/0306422019895724

JOURNALIST GAD LERNER attended the annual conference of Matteo Salvini's League Party in the northern Italian town of Pontida this September. Salvini, until recently deputy prime minister, had spent the summer on Italian beaches, where he was filmed DJ-ing and escalating his bombastic, hardman rhetoric against journalists – hinting that a critical reporter might have paedophile tendencies, and suggesting that the press was biased against his party.

A crowd of Salvini fans had gathered to make clear Lerner was not welcome in Pontida.

"Go away! What are you doing here?" some were filmed saying.

"Clown!" others added.

"Piece of shit!"

"You're not Italian, you Jew!"

On the same day, Salvini supporters attacked La Repubblica video-journalist Antonio Nasso, punching his camera.

Afterwards, Salvini chose to put his weight behind the attacks with what appeared to be, at least, partial support. Among other things, he said Lerner "was looking for it" and that "these are not journalists but ... slanderers".

The episode is symptomatic of how Salvini's sardonic jeers and strongman rhetoric against reporters might be encouraging anti-journalist feelings among his supporters.

It's a situation that is not exclusive to Italy. Strongmen leaders around the world regularly attack the media – we live in an era in which critical stories are dubbed as "fake news", journalists are branded as "enemies" and political rallies are dominated by chants against news organisations.

But what has happened in Italy should be a salutary lesson for the world of journalism. The low standards that are reflected too often within the country's media mean that Salvini has been pushing at an open door when it comes to building on public distrust of journalists.

"Italians already didn't have any trust in the media," said Leonardo Bianchi, a news editor at Vice Italy who often reports on far-right and neo-fascist groups, and the author of La Gente (The People), a book on resentment among Italians. "Some haven't had any trust in them for a very long time – for many different, and in some cases right, reasons," he said. "Salvini merely exploits this lack of trust for electoral gains."

Trust in the media is "particularly low" in Italy, according to the 2019 Digital News Report by the Reuters Institute for the Study of Journalism. The report put trust in the media at 40% and found that only 33% of Italians thought the media scrutinised the powerful well – the second-lowest score in Europe after Hungary. To put these figures into context, in the October regional election in Umbria, Salvini's Lega party won 37% of the vote, and the far-right Brothers of Italy (FdI) party added another 10%. These parties appear to be held in higher esteem than journalists.

Trust in the media is "particularly low" in Italy

Many observers think that to win back public trust, Italian media might have to go back to basics.

Lorenzo Pregliasco, co-founder of polling and communications consultancies Quorum and YouTrend, is among those who think the media have to fix some bad habits to be more credible. "I think the media can improve in doing the job people expect them to do," he said. They need to avoid publishing "unverified stories, fabricated quotes and fabricated interviews".

Some of these are widely accepted practices. A few depend on a lack of journalistic rigour – it's not unusual for newspapers to use edited or fabricated quotes in headlines to sum up somebody's position. In some cases, they opt for clickbait headlines, hasty production and verification, and poor judgment. For example, it's common for newspapers across the political spectrum to republish unbalanced and unfiltered clips from Salvini's Facebook Live broadcasts.

"We have been carrying around many of these problems for a very long time," said Arianna Ciccone, co-founder of the International Journalism Festival in Perugia. "There has never been a 'golden age' of Italian journalism in this sense."

She says that fixing these bad practices would be the best place to start to address both low trust levels and attacks plaguing Italian media. "The true defensive weapon against politicians' attacks [on the media] is quality journalism," she said, defining "quality journalism" as accurate, in-depth and transparent reporting. This appears to be a low bar. "Simply verifying a story before publishing is quality journalism," she added.

Bianchi, of Vice Italy, agrees. To fight →

ABOVE: Salvini speaks at a national demonstration against the new government in October 2019

SALVINI: "GETS MORE AIRTIME THAN ANY OTHER POLITICIAN"

MATTEO SALVINI WAS filmed uttering slightly unexpected words a year ago while he was still the interior minister. "I'm a journalist," he told reporters. "I appreciate freedom of thought, of speech and criticism." A few seconds later, he expressed "solidarity with journalists who do their job well".

It might be hard to reconcile these words with his better-known, scornful attacks on journalists. Isn't he the guy who praised Vladimir Putin, Viktor Orbán and Recep Tayyip Erdogan – not exactly Europe's champions of freedom of expression? Doesn't he have a track record of attacks on critical reporters? Doesn't he rely on Facebook Live to bypass journalistic scrutiny?

Yet, according to reporters who have followed Salvini for years, his more "friendly" face might be as important as his strongman persona to understand his relationship with the media.

"I see two faces," said Alessandro Franzi, a reporter who followed Salvini's rise between 2012 and 2018 and co-wrote a book profiling Salvini titled Il Militante (The Campaigner).

"Onstage and in front of his supporters, Salvini needs to attack journalists as 'enemies of the people'. This is the strongman face he wears at rallies or during his Facebook Live broadcasts, where he launches tirades against reporters and the "partisan" press, which he portrays as constantly attacking him. "His attacks on journalists are part of his game and the rhetoric that holds up his type of leadership."

His authoritarian tendencies have also surfaced when he tries to condition the Italian media landscape. For example, he pushed to appoint journalist Marcello Foa, who peddled absurd conspiracy theories, including some about Hillary Clinton and Satanic rites, as head of Italy's public broadcaster Rai.

But on the other side, Salvini has excellent ties with the media that he "has cultivated since his very early days", according to Franzi. "Offstage, he is a leader who takes everyone's questions because, in the end, he needs the media."

The good relationships pay dividends. Salvini is a constant fixture on Italian TV, playing the role of man of the people, drinking wine, eating traditional food, praising Jesus and speaking plainly – so much so that people such as Bianchi argue that the media give Salvini preferential treatment.

Italy's communications regulator Autorità per le Garanzie nelle Comunicazioni found that Salvini enjoyed more Italian TV news airtime in July 2019 than any other politician – 225 minutes. His closest competitor was the Five Star Movement's Luigi Di Maio, who failed to reach 100.

→ back against attacks and attempts to discredit reporters, "we must work upstream", he said. "We must be credible and be perceived to be."

Improving the standard of journalism in Italy wouldn't by itself prevent the macho behaviour of people such as Salvini. But it would make it harder for the media to be such an easy target for populists.

A few outlets, such as Il Post, have carved out their niche around more sober headlines and factual reporting, but their reach remains limited compared with the mainstream press.

And while scale and financial constraints make it hard for Italian publications to emulate the journalism produced by The Guardian or The New York Times, Ciccone believes Italian media could be inspired by smaller operations that produce accurate in-depth reporting around the world – she cites Mother Jones and ProPublica in the USA and Mediapart in France.

Asked if anyone was going in the right direction, Ciccone replied: "There are many

It's common for newspapers across the political spectrum to republish clips from Salvini's Facebook Live broadcasts, unbalanced and unfiltered

excellent journalists in Italy." She named a few. Any publications? There is silence, then a nervous chuckle, then another pause. "No comment." ⊗

__Alessio Perrone__ is an Italian journalist from Milan

Macho, macho man

In Tanzania, tough-guy politics is putting democratic gains at risk. **Neema Komba** reports

48(04): 45/47 | DOI: 10.1177/0306422019895725

A TRICKLE-DOWN MACHO LEADERSHIP style known as *kujimwabafai* is increasingly popular in Tanzania. The term is used to define public officials who abuse their power and treat others unfairly in order to appear more powerful: people who disregard the rule of law and embrace authoritarianism in an attempt to gain favour with the current president, John Magufuli.

In October this year, Paul Makonda, the Dar es Salaam regional commissioner, instructed Idris Sultan to report to the central police station after the popular comedian posted a "face swap" with the president on social media.

Sultan was held for impersonation under the 2015 Cybercrimes Act, a law which also impinges upon freedom of expression.

Tanzania, a largely patriarchal society yearning for development, chose the macho Magufuli as president in its last election, and his ego is getting in the way of the country's freedoms. Tired of rampant corruption, believed to have been the result of the laissez-faire style of his predecessor, Tanzanians wanted a decisive leader who would fight the ills plaguing the country. Nicknamed the Bulldozer, Magufuli set out to clean up the country.

While some of the changes he has brought have been welcomed, and long overdue, democracy has become a casualty in the process.

His supporters see him as an infallible leader who cannot err, and his word has sometimes been taken as law. Magufuli's government has been keen to receive praise for doing its job, but on the flipside it is reluctant to receive any criticism and is waging a war on dissent.

As we went to press, journalist Erick Kabendera – who was arrested on trumped-up charges in August – was still awaiting trial. His court case has been postponed eight times already.

But Kabendera's whereabouts are, at least, known. Others, such as Azory Gwanda – who has been missing since November 2017 – have disappeared completely.

Recent reports by Amnesty International and Human Rights Watch show that civic society, political parties and the press face varying forms of suppression within the country. The government has created a climate of fear among its citizens, who now believe that the only way to be safe is to be silent.

"Before pursuing a story, you ask yourself if 600 words are worth the repercussions," said Khalifa Said, a political writer at The Citizen newspaper, in an interview with Index. Said's comment reflects the current reality for journalists in Tanzania.

"No one has to beat down your door to tell you not to publish certain things," he said. "When you see repressive laws against media and journalism pass, when you see your colleagues arrested and newspapers suspended, you know you have to tread very lightly. You censor yourself."

Said has first-hand experience of this. In February 2019, The Citizen was suspended for seven days simply for running a story about the declining value of the Tanzanian shilling against the US dollar.

Laws have also enshrined the assault on free speech.

Legislation such as the Media Services Act of 2016, which was deemed by the East African Court of Justice to be against freedom of →

Before pursuing a story, you ask yourself if 600 words are worth the repercussions

→ the press, has made journalists reluctant to speak out.

Said was willing to talk to me. But when I approach other journalists to ask about their experiences in Tanzania, most of them are afraid to speak on the record.

One confided that this was "because there is no freedom of expression".

And this self-censorship isn't exclusive to journalists, either.

"You can't talk about everything," said Gadi Ramadhani, a visual artist, curator and founder of KokoTEN studios. By everything, he means not least Magufuli and his government – unless, of course, you are going to talk positively about them.

Visual artists, filmmakers and musicians face censorship from the National Arts Council, which has a mandate to ban content it deems inappropriate. What's inappropriate could be anyone's guess. It is not always clear what content could get someone in trouble. And because there isn't a directive that says what can and cannot be said, no one really knows what can land them in trouble, so they err on the side of caution.

The government has banned political songs in the past, but visual artists enjoy relatively more freedom due to the more ambiguous nature of the art form. In October, Ramadhani exhibited Everlast – a body of work that depicts the dire situation of Tanzanian democracy – at the Alliance Française in Dar es Salaam.

"I chose the name carefully, to let the audience arrive at their own meaning. Visual art is subject to interpretation; therefore, I cannot be held responsible for someone else's interpretation of my work," he told Index.

The level of censorship may also depend on the level of influence the artists and their art have on the masses.

Dotto Rangimoto, a Tanzanian poet and the 2017 winner of the Mabati Cornell Prize for African Literature, believes poetry and literary arts – which aren't very popular in the country – retain some freedom of expression.

The National Arts Council does not have a mandate to censor literature, but Rangimoto,

Some gender activists have been calling out the president's mostly male appointments to positions of authority with the hashtag #TeuziDume (male appointments)

who has written and shared online poems such as Mfalme Nakutukana (I Curse the King) and Dereva Kipofu (The Blind Driver), still gets a few private warnings from people.

"They would call you and say, 'You are headed down the wrong path my friend'."

These warnings from strangers and loved ones to journalists and artists are justified. But perhaps such an overt show of male authoritarian politics could be used for political advantage. Some gender activists have been calling out the president's mostly male appointments to positions of authority with the hashtag *#TeuziDume* (male appointments). Despite having a female vice-president, the number of women in leadership is disproportionately lower than men.

Historically, Tanzanian women have been left out of political and non-political decision-making positions – a situation which led to the passage of affirmative action laws in 1985 to reduce the gender gap. *#TeuziDume* serves as a reminder that the country is still leaving women out.

Rangimoto has a suggestion to remedy this macho trend: "We need more women in politics."

But as Tanzania heads towards its 2020 general elections, it won't be surprising if this trend continues. Magufuli remains the most likely winner, and if the political space remains hostile, and free speech is totally muzzled, Tanzania's peace and democracy will be in peril. ⊗

Neema Komba is an award-winning Tanzanian writer and poet

Putin's pushbacks

Vladimir Putin's macho image works only when he can give the people what they want, argues **Andrey Arkhangelskiy**

48(04): 48/49 I DOI: 10.1177/0306422019895726

WHEN VLADIMIR PUTIN was first elected Russian president in March 2000, he presented an image of the perfect husband and father: he didn't drink, he didn't smoke, he was in good physical shape, he had a degree and he was practical. His comparative youth (he was 48) also seemed revolutionary in a country where leaders had usually been ageing and suffering from poor health. In the mass consciousness, Putin was accepted as "a second Mikhail Gorbachev" (who had also been significantly younger than previous leaders). Unlike Gorbachev, however, it soon became clear that Putin had a macho side.

At the time, there was an overwhelming desire for law and order. But, paradoxically, the popular urge for a strong president did not mean people wanted to turn away from democracy. (From 1985 to 1999, under Gorbachev and Boris Yeltsin, the country had experienced an unprecedented sense of freedom.)

During the 1980s years of perestroika, censorship on television and in newspapers was reduced, and people heard and read things that could not have been said previously. After 1991, the country moved from socialism to a private economy. It became possible to travel abroad, to buy and sell, to make money. It was a hurricane of freedom.

However ardent their love was for Putin as a strong leader, the people certainly did not intend to give up their freedoms.

But giving up some political freedom so as to bring order to the country was an unspoken idea in the Kremlin during the first decade of the 21st century. Today the Kremlin is putting forward another unofficial idea – the notion that Russia is surrounded by enemies, so people have to temporarily forego their personal liberties. It's a different argument with the same goal and it shows how limiting social and political freedom in Russia was never dictated by genuine threats. The authorities need these threats to achieve some tactical target, such as getting rid of political opponents and not giving critics a platform.

And Putin is hamming up his macho side. At a meeting last year with the Federal Assembly, he devoted more than a third of his speech to the latest developments of new nuclear weapons. This year, in an interview with The Financial Times, he stated that "the liberal idea is out of date". His rhetoric is becoming increasingly militaristic and conservative.

Russian people have appeared indifferent to infringements on their liberties. Sometimes they have even been impressed by the state's macho style. On occasions they are ready to forget about their poverty-stricken situation and to take pride in an apparent victory by the state on the international stage. At times they may even be pleased with the state's use of violence.

But we cannot say that the people actively demanded that free speech or political freedom be limited. The closure in the early 2000s of independent TV companies NTV, TV-6 and TVS did not increase Putin's popularity. Neither did he become more popular when he shut other independent media outlets in 2012-16. But while none of this affected his image, it was only because the Kremlin tried to do this on the quiet. People don't support restrictions on freedom, so the authorities don't announce bans.

> *But, paradoxically, the popular urge for a strong president did not mean people wanted to turn away from democracy*

The Kremlin has also relied very successfully on subconscious totalitarian stereotypes, which are strong in Russia: cynicism, indifference and the acceptance of state violence against individuals. The Kremlin uses household conservatism and prejudice to consolidate a majority. This is why the LGBT movement could not have mass support in Russia. However, this topic did not seriously worry Russians – until it was talked about on television.

The authorities play on the fact that the majority of Russians still have only a vague idea about what democracy and freedom really mean. There has been no broad discussion within society about what actually happened to the country in 1991 (in reality, the country experienced a bourgeois revolution). This means that many people still have never really experienced political freedom or freedom of speech.

But this doesn't mean that people who live in Russia have no sense of freedom. Opinion polls conducted by the non-partisan Levada Centre show that half the population believe that having independent media and criticism of the state is normal.

It's true that the pro-Putin media occasionally demand the closure of opposition media, because "they slander Russia", but such a view is not considered official. Indeed, the Kremlin has never formally denied that there should be another point of view. A formal ban on the independent press would officially signal that Russia had joined the ranks of authoritarian states, which is something the Kremlin doesn't want. The authorities understand, too, that a new restriction on freedom of speech could lead to mass protests.

And despite its macho style, the Kremlin does sometimes behave cautiously. For example, attempts in 2018 by the state to block social media site Telegram ended in farce. The company refused to hand over its encryption keys and the authorities had to back down.

The macho style, which does not bring any improvement to people's economic wellbeing, cannot last long. According to official statistics, 20 million people in Russia today are living below the poverty line. The economic situation for the rest of the population is not improving, and the state continues to increase its share of the country's economy.

The raising of the pension age in 2018 to 65 for men and 60 for women was an important turning point. For the first time there was a mass vote for opposition candidates at the elections for regional governors. People went to the polls with the express intention of voting for any candidate other than those who represented the state. And for the first time the Kremlin could do nothing about it. Since then, trust in the ruling party and even in Putin himself has been steadily declining, which is reflected in opinion polls.

Perhaps the macho style is no longer working? There are no clear-cut answers. We can merely affirm one thing: limiting political and social freedom has never added to Putin's popularity, in spite of the cliché that Russian society likes any ban or limit on freedom. Just because people have been indifferent to this for a long time doesn't mean that they like it. ⊗

Translated by **Stephen Dalziel**

***Andrey Arkhangelskiy** is a journalist and editor based in Moscow*

ABOVE: People stand in front of a figure of Vladimir Putin, marked with the slogans "military" and "economic", at a carnival in Dusseldorf, Germany

GLOBAL VIEW

Trying to shut down women

Many female members of the UK parliament are standing down as the level of abuse they receive rises. **Jodie Ginsberg** talks about enforcing the law and standing up in support of them

48(04): 50/51 | DOI: 10.1177/0306422019895764

BELOW: Letter sent to Stella Creasy, currently standing to be a Labour MP

"**WHAT BECOMETH A** woman best, and first of all? Silence. What second? Silence. What third? Silence. What fourth? Silence. Yea, if a man should aske me till Domes daie I would still crie silence, silence" – Thomas Wilson, the Arte of Rhetorique, 1560

At the time of writing, as we enter the final stages of a UK general election that follows three years of bitter political fighting, the attempts to silence women who enter that fray have come once again into sharp focus. The "art of rhetoric" that Wilson wrote of in 1560 seems, in 2019, to consist mainly of personal attacks, and the verbal attacks on women are often the most vicious.

MP after MP has talked about the almost daily slew of violent threats they receive via social media: threats of rape, threats of violence towards their families, death threats. Ahead of this election campaign, 20 female MPs announced they would be standing down, and many cited the abuse they received as a reason for doing so. One of them was Nicky Morgan, a member of the cabinet, who referred to the impact on her family and "the other sacrifices involved in and the abuse for doing the job of a modern MP".

Diane Abbott, who is currently standing for re-election, is a particular target for abuse. "It's the volume of it which makes it so debilitating, so corrosive and so upsetting. It's the sheer volume. And the sheer level of hatred that people are showing," she told Amnesty researchers studying abuse faced by female politicians during the last general election. Abbott received death threats and rape threats on a daily basis. In the six weeks leading up to 8 June 2017, the date of that election, Amnesty found that Abbott was the victim of 45% of all abusive tweets sent to female MPs. She received 4,512 of these tweets, and because deleted tweets or messages sent from accounts that had subsequently been suspended were not counted, the true figure could be much higher.

And the abuse doesn't take place only online, although that is where it is most prevalent.

Stella Creasy, who is a campaigner on abortion law and is standing to be a Labour London MP as we go to press, was met by billboard posters in her London constituency showing foetuses and the words "Stop Stella" splashed across them. While the advertisers argued they had every right to highlight – and object to – a politician's political stance, "Stop Stella" can take on an ominous secondary meaning in this febrile atmosphere.

A man also tried to smash the office window of Labour MP, Jess Phillips, shouting "fascist".

Only three years ago, a female MP, Jo Cox, was murdered on the streets of her West Yorkshire constituency during a referendum campaign, so MPs have every justification for feeling nervous as they canvas for votes in the dark in this election period.

Since Cox's death, many have made changes to their lives. Abbott told Grazia magazine: "I used to go everywhere on my own; now my staff make an effort to accompany me to places where I didn't require a chaperone before."

Faced with a relentless onslaught of credible threats – not to mention the personal, "lower level" of abuse that is regularly dished out – it is hardly surprising that many choose to pull back from public life altogether. My own MP, Heidi Allen, said she would not contest the

December 2019 election, writing in her resignation speech that she was "exhausted by the invasion into [her] privacy and the nastiness and intimidation that has become commonplace".

It is not just MPs who face this daily level of aggression. Other high-profile figures – including journalists – are targeted for regular abuse. Indian journalist Rana Ayyub receives death and rape threats following her investigation into riots that killed at least 1,000 people in 2002 and in which Narendra Modi, the current prime minister, was accused of complicity. Her social media accounts and phone have been inundated with messages urging people to gang-rape her. Her phone number and address were posted online.

Ayyub continues to report. But for many others, such abuse is impossible to stomach. The result is the withdrawing from public life of vital voices, and that is hugely damaging for democracy. Without voices, we lose power, and that leads to political (and other) decisions being made that negatively impact the voiceless and entrench existing power structures.

The two options we seem to be presented with as solutions are no answers at all. The first suggests that those who choose careers in public life should simply grow a thicker skin or – as one participant at a conference on this issue once memorably told me – learn to SITFU ("suck it the fuck up"). This is easier said than done, especially if you're the one on the receiving end of violent and credible threats to your personal safety and that of your loved ones.

But neither is banning all hateful speech an answer, not least because "hateful speech" has a tendency to incorporate ever widening definitions that rapidly scoop up what is generally considered to be lawful and legitimate speech.

So what should be done? Well, first let's enforce the laws we already have. In the UK, as in most countries, there are plenty of laws that deal with threats of violence, yet few reports of such threats end in conviction. Focusing energy on dealing with those individuals who directly threaten violence – a far smaller proportion than those who engage in legal but distasteful speech – is a far better use of resources, including police resources, than attempting to net an ever-widening shoal of speech. The imprisoning of the men involved in a plot to kill MP Rosie Cooper is an example of how these laws can be used to prosecute and protect.

Secondly, we need to be better allies. When we see people targeted with abusive speech, we should speak up in their defence. Abusers try to silence their opponents by isolating them. Standing with people targeted and threatened for their opinions – even when you disagree with those opinions – shows they are not alone.

Finally, we should start taking responsibility for how we engage with others, and remembering that all those who engage in public are human beings. Civic discourse doesn't have to be civil – and often it absolutely should not be – but it should never involve threats of violence. ⊗

ABOVE: A service commemorating murdered MP Jo Cox

BELOW: Email sent to Jess Phillips, currently standing to be a Labour MP

Shut it phillips
We hope you have lost your seat
Because you are a back stabbing goby cow
Your fucking ugly fat cow
What your husband see's in you is beyond
Use ever thought of hanging your self or
Putting a rope around your neck go on do it
And make people happy, perhaps you could
So shut the fuck up.

Sent from Mail for Windows 10

Jodie Ginsberg is the Index CEO

跟毛主席在大风大浪中前进

红卫兵

毛泽东
ZE DONG

赠给革命军人

PICTURED: A book vendor at his stall in the Panjiayuan antiques market in Beijing

IN FOCUS

54 DIRTY INDUSTY, DIRTY TACTICS
STEPHEN WOODMAN
Protesting against mining in Central and
South America can be a fatal endeavor

57 MUSIC TO YEMEN'S EARS
LAURA SILVIA BATTAGLIA
When musical expression is repressed, a
thriving orchestra is a revolutinary act

61 PLAY ON JEMIMAH STEINFELD
Opera singer **Jamie Barton** and music
director **Lidiya Yankovskaya** on defying
oppression through music

64 THE FINAL CHAPTER? KAROLINE KAN
The forced closure of a Beijing bookshop
exemplifies intellectual censorship in China

66 WORKING IT OUT STEVEN BOROWIEC
Activists battle the ingrained culture of
workplace bullying in South Korea

69 PROTEST WORKS RACHAEL JOLLEY
AND JEMIMAH STEINFELD

Radu Vancu and **Dóra Papp** on how slow and
steady protest techniques win the race

**73 IT'S A LITTLE BIT SILENT, THIS
FEELING INSIDE** SILVIA NORTES
In Spain suicide remains an issue shrouded in
a counter-productive silence

Dirty industry, dirty tactics

Anti-mining activists are risking their lives to speak out in Brazil, Mexico and Peru, reports **Stephen Woodman**

48(04): 54/56 | DOI: 10.1177/0306422019895463

AN ENVIRONMENTAL ACTIVIST lives in constant fear in northern Mexico. An indigenous leader is stabbed to death and tossed in a river in the Brazilian jungle. A regional governor is given a six-year prison sentence by a court in Peru. Separate fates tied by a single thread: all three had opposed mining projects.

The extractive industries – and their devastating impact on the environment – will be on the agenda when officials convene for the 2019 United Nations Climate Change Conference in December in Spain, under the presidency of the government of Chile. But outside diplomatic circles, publicly discussing mining activities has become a perilous task in Latin America.

According to Global Witness, an environmental watchdog, mining was the deadliest sector for land defenders in 2018: 43 people were murdered after standing up to mining interests, and 11 of those killings occurred in Latin America.

Victoria Tauli-Corpuz, the UN special rapporteur on the rights of indigenous peoples, told Index that the persecution of environmental defenders did not involve just physical violence. Activists are also facing hostile rhetoric from politicians, while courts are increasingly reinterpreting laws to silence defenders.

In my visits to various parts of Latin America, I have seen an increase in harassment against land rights defenders, Tauli-Corpuz said.

For Mexican activist Isela González, this crisis is also a personal tragedy. A nurse-turned-anthropologist, González has spent more than two decades campaigning for the rights of indigenous groups living in the mountains of Chihuahua state in the country's north-west.

The Rarámuri indigenous inhabitants of this region are struggling to defend their territory from a range of predatory outsiders, including corrupt politicians, criminal gangs and international mining companies keen to exploit the land.

González has suffered multiple death threats, despite living in a city outside the community. "It's difficult to go out anywhere," she told Index. "I'm always worried about people following me in the street."

The risks are so great that González has registered in Mexico's federal programme to protect human-rights defenders and journalists. The state provides panic buttons for her office, steel doors for her home and armed escorts to accompany her on visits to indigenous communities.

For González's fellow campaigners within the tribal territories, the risks are even greater. In October last year, the indigenous land defender Julián Carrillo was shot dead in the mountains after years of campaigning against destructive activities such as mining. He was the sixth member

The exclusive focus on criminal gangs obscures the role of the mining companies themselves, who routinely offer extortion payments to gangs

of his family to be murdered in two years.

As Carrillo was also enrolled in the federal protection programme, Amnesty International has concluded that the Mexican state failed to guarantee protection for his legitimate defence of his ancestral territory.

"The security provisions for the defenders in the community are totally inadequate," González said. "They live in regions with no access to security support. They have to wait between six and 10 hours for the police to arrive."

The presence of organised crime in the region massively compounds the dangers for defenders. But the exclusive focus on criminal gangs obscures the role of the mining companies themselves, who routinely offer extortion payments to gangs. According to Amnesty International, Carrillo spoke at a community assembly just days before his murder. He specifically voiced concern that the granting of a new mining concession on tribal territory would increase violence and criminality.

Indigenous groups in Brazil have also been rocked by a series of recent incursions into their territory. In July, dozens of armed gold-miners entered a protected Amazonian village occupied by members of the Wajãpi tribe in the northern state of Amapá. Four days earlier, Emyra Wajãpi, a local leader, had been fatally stabbed and thrown in a river in the same region. Indigenous councillors blamed the gold-miners for the murder. Randolfe Rodrigues, a state senator for Amapá, held Brazil's president, Jair Bolsonaro, responsible.

"The Wajãpi villagers are terrified, both by the episode with Emyra and with the threats from the federal government," said Rodrigues.

Bolsonaro has promised to open the Amazon to business. He wants to leave Convention 169 – a treaty with the International Labour Organisation – and begin mining without consulting indigenous communities.

ABOVE: A woman protests against Brazilian mining company Vale after a dam collapsed in January 2019, which killed hundreds

The risks are so great that González has registered in Mexico's federal programme to protect human-rights defenders and journalists

→ With Bolsanaro's position clear, illegal gold-miners and other land raiders have mobilised. According to Brazil's Indigenous Missionary Council, a Catholic church group, 153 indigenous territories were raided in the first nine months of the year. That figure is more than double the total for the whole of 2017.

Bolsonaro has consistently portrayed indigenous groups and their supporters as anti-development. He has complained that they are encouraged to live "like animals in zoos". He has also tried to undermine indigenous leaders by voicing doubts that Wajãpi was murdered.

"[The president's] discourse reinforced the idea that it was all a scam," said Charly Sanches, an environmental activist from Amapá. "Seeking to discredit indigenous people has become routine practice since Bolsonaro's election."

Brazil is one of the world's deadliest countries for environmental defenders. Indigenous groups in isolated areas are particularly vulnerable to hostile rhetoric and the violence it inspires.

Confrontations involving lawyers rather than gunmen have also become common in Latin America. In Peru, authorities have begun to reinterpret laws to punish the opponents of mining projects. This August, a court sentenced Walter Aduviri, the governor of the Puno region, to six years in prison and a fine equivalent to $600,000 for his role in the protests against a mining concession in the area in 2011. Anger at the refusal to consult the Aymara indigenous community drove the protests, which led to clashes with police in which five people died. The backlash prompted the Peruvian government to cancel their concession to Bear Creek, a Canadian mining corporation.

Aduviri was eventually convicted of disturbing the peace. The 39-year-old was singled out as a "non-executive perpetrator", suggesting he incited crimes which others carried out. In the past, this legal concept has mostly been used in cases of crimes against humanity and terrorism.

Pablo Abdo, a lawyer from the Institute for the Study of Andean Cultures in Puno, said: "Social protest revolves around three rights: freedom of assembly, freedom of expression and freedom to petition. But the law is being reinterpreted to criminalise that protest."

Aduviri was elected governor of Puno in October last year, despite spending the campaign season as a fugitive. A judge ordered his arrest in August. Aduviri's lawyers plan to fight the sentence on the grounds that there is no evidence linking him to any crime.

However, Abdo said the case had already discouraged other land defenders.

"Right now, there are indigenous people in Puno who are scared to assume a [leadership] role," he said. "They are afraid that if they are visible they will be charged as criminals."

Across Latin America, mining operations present an existential threat to the rights and freedoms of indigenous people. The UN addressed these issues for the first time in the latest report by its Intergovernmental Panel on Climate Change. The report acknowledged that indigenous people offer sustainable stewardship of environmental resources. It said strengthening the recognition of these groups represented a proven strategy for slowing the climate crisis.

Alice Harrison, a spokesperson for Global Witness, said the UN report recognised that often-maligned indigenous groups offered a healthy model of existence.

"The irony is that many of these [mining operations] that are causing killings and criminalisation of whole communities are being posited as development projects," Harrison said. "But when we talk to [indigenous] groups, they are saying: 'What kind of development is this exactly?'" ⊗

Stephen Woodman *is the contributing editor for Index on Censorship in Mexico. He is based in Guadalajara*

Music to Yemen's ears

After years of music being banned by the Houthis in Yemen, a new orchestra is attracting a squad of young women. **Laura Silvia Battaglia** speaks to the director and its students

48(04): 57/60 I DOI: 10.1177/0306422019895464

THE PERFORMANCE OPENS with Trevor Jones's iconic instrumental piece, the soundtrack to the Oscar-winning film The Last of the Mohicans.

"This piece is part of our teaching programme," explains Abdullah Ali al-Dubai, director of a new orchestra in Yemen, before giving the starting nod to his student orchestra of violinists, guitarists and oud players. The tone is a little off, but the phrasing is smooth.

"It's a perfect practice piece for a young string orchestra," the director comments humbly, smiling warmly when the piece comes to an end.

The performance may have been a teaching exercise but, figuratively-speaking, al-Dubai could also be the last of the Mohicans for his own generation – namely, a member of the 1970s Yemeni national orchestra, which was disbanded in the early 1980s. Yemen once had a highly respected musical tradition but the number of performances has plummeted and concert halls remain empty. In the city of Sana'a and northern Yemeni villages, Houthi militias have regularly stormed events – even weddings – seizing instruments and placing those playing music in public under temporary arrest. They describe music as an "impure and corrupt form of expression not to be encouraged". But for the first time in years, music is coming back to Yemen, with al-Dubai's orchestra in Sana'a marking the re-emergence.

What started with just 10 students a year ago has already grown to a 40-strong squad, all of whom are keen to exercise their musical free expression. But they still encounter harassment when out in public. Fourteen-year-old Ahlam Abdul Wahab, who grew up being ridiculed on the streets, has found a refuge in the orchestra.

"If people catch sight of my violin in its case when I'm out, they insult me. They hiss and yell, 'Hey girl, you there with the oud, why don't you come and play at my wedding?' I hate them but there's nothing I can do about it."

When she goes to music lessons, Abdul Wahab has to hide her violin in a bag for fear of being attacked. Her love of music has become a battle of wills – a personal civil war in war-torn Yemen.

"I play and I want to learn to play for a variety of reasons. The first one is to rid Yemeni society of the idea that musicians are servants, from the lowest classes of society. It's a belief we've carried with us, especially in northern Yemen, since the rule of the imams, before the republic and after Ottoman rule. The second is that it's [seen as] immoral for girls to play music – this is not true. My family and the musical director are both behind me and are proving that we can."

Al-Dubai, who is proud of the fact the orchestra has many women in it, said: "[Women] have the potential to bring great change to society. The more women receive musical training, the more men will be affected by their enthusiasm. Music is an instrument of peace and we need peace in Yemen. Peace alone."

How has al-Dubai managed to escape the Houthis' grip? He says a deal was struck a year ago in which he was allowed to run the orchestra as long as it never gave public →

If people catch sight of my violin in its case when I'm out, they insult me. They hiss and yell

Music is an instrument of peace and we need peace in Yemen

→ performances, and it operated only in the academy, inside the courtyard of the academy or at home. This compromise, for al-Dubai, is currently his only option if he wants to play and teach music.

"It's a big, unexpected, amazing step," he said of the orchestra's growing success, adding that about 50 people are applying to join the orchestra each year – a significant number for Sana'a.

Still, al-Dubai is nostalgic for the days of old.

"I grew up a musician in the Yemen of Ibrahim al-Hamdi and was in a band called Ibrahim Mohammed al-Hamdi. For six long years, we were trained by musicians from North Korea. They had all studied at the institute and taught us everything they knew about western music," he said.

Al-Dubai smiles contentedly at the memory. "There were 27 of us – 25 men and two women. Television was black and white. We toured the whole country and played in every province because the television didn't reach beyond Sana'a. International tours followed soon after. We even went to the United States."

Glimpses of these golden years are captured in the pictures taken by photographer Abdulrahman al-Ghabri.

"I was a personal friend of the blind poet Abdullah al-Baradouni," al-Ghabri told Index. "I toured with the national orchestra, I photographed the great vocalist and oud player Ali al-Anisi. They were different times: we were free to express ourselves, to live according to the traditions of our culture. But this all changed after the 1970s."

For al-Dubai, life without music is not only sadder, it is less hopeful, and hope is in desperate

CREDIT: Mohammed Al-Sayaghi/Reuters

need in Yemen right now. There is hope among his students, though.

Mohammad Sultan al-Yousifi, who sees himself as both a poet and a musician, said: "The director al-Dubai has gone to great lengths to set up the orchestra. We want to pick

up the baton and grow Yemeni music until we can perform it in public. So what if we can't do it now? In the future we will: for now, it's important to prepare the ground."

Fairuz Dhaif Allah agrees with her younger colleague. At 40, she's the only adult female in the orchestra and the music school has been a breath of fresh air for her.

"I studied music when I was young. I learned to play the piano. Then I married, I had children and all sorts of things happened to the city. Ironically, the war now offers us this

ABOVE: Yemeni girls, part of Abdullah Ali al-Dubai's orchestra, play guitars at the cultural centre in Sana'a

glimmer of hope. I play oud in this tiny orchestra. In part I enjoy it and in part I think that you have to start from the little things to counter the ignorance and sexism of our society."

Al-Dubai's ambitions don't end here. He wants to make sure that other kinds of music, not just classical, become accepted. And he already has people who want to channel this vision.

Ahlam's 13-year-old sister would like to learn freestyle. Her inspiration is Yemeni rapper Amaani Yahya, who rose to fame as a teenager during the Arab Spring of 2011 and now lives in exile in the USA. In order to become even remotely as famous as her hero, Ahlam's sister

has learned how to improvise on the keyboard.

"But the next step is to get away from here, just like Amaani," she told Index.

Maybe exile won't be needed if orchestras such as al-Dubai's rise in prominence and put music back on Yemen's map. ⊗

*Translated by **Denise Muir***

***Laura Silvia Battaglia** is a contributing editor (Yemen and Iraq) for Index on Censorship*

Play on

Can music be a form of resistance? **Jemimah Steinfeld** talks to opera singer **Jamie Barton** and music director **Lidiya Yankovskaya** about how

48(04): 61/63 I DOI: 10.1177/0306422019895465

"**WITHOUT MUSIC, LIFE** would be a mistake," said Friedrich Nietzsche.

Alas, the German philosopher's view is not shared by everyone.

Since time eternal, music has been banned for many reasons – "moral pollution" being a common charge – with Index frequently campaigning for, and championing, musicians who are censored.

This year has been no exception. From the sentencing of a rapper in Morocco this November to one year in prison (linked to a song he co-wrote) to the musicians who are seeing their work banned in China for speaking out in favour of the Hong Kong protesters, censorship of musicians is alive – and thriving – around the globe.

And yet, as shown by Laura Silvia Battaglia's piece (p.57-60) discussing the emergence of an orchestra in Yemen after years of a musical blackout, there are glimmers of hope.

For this issue, we spoke to two other artists who are challenging the limits of musical free expression. Opera singer Jamie Barton, from Georgia, USA, says she has people telling her to get off stage because of her liberal views. Her response? Programming as many female composers as her time allows and headlining the BBC's Last Night of the Proms this year with Pride flag in hand.

Conductor and music director Lidiya Yankovskaya, who originally comes from Russia, has not been affected by censorship in the country in the same way as musicians such as Pussy Riot, but her experience as a refugee led to her founding the Refugee Orchestra Project. Through this she works with people who lived in countries, such as Afghanistan, at a time when playing music could result in instruments being smashed, beatings or imprisonment.

Both musicians are working in the USA, where their messages aren't always well received. But they're unwilling to be silenced and instead are amplifying their own voices and the voices of the marginalised. And they're producing great music in the process.

Nietzsche would be happy. ⊗

Jemimah Steinfeld is deputy editor at Index on Censorship

DISCORDANT NOTES

THERE'S AN INEQUALITY in the cultivation of female voices in the music world, opera singer Jamie Barton tells Index, adding that they're "a completely untapped reserve".

The award-winning opera singer, who closed this year's BBC Proms concerts in London and has sellout performances coming up in the UK and the USA, is passionate about giving women a voice.

And she says she would support an initiative focusing on recovering "lost" female composers.

"Just going to the Wikipedia page I knew about 1% of the women composers they had listed and I do this for my job," she said.

"Sometimes the compositions of women of the past are so unknown that you have to find library collections that might have the rare reprints available to be able to look through their music because it's unavailable for purchase. At this point, there is a lot of extra effort that goes into finding music by women of past eras, and that presents a hurdle for many performers."

Barton's own voice – which has been described as velvety rich – is at its boldest when she's rallying the marginalised.

With a nose stud and hair that varies from hot pink to purple, the 37-year-old waved the Pride flag at the Proms as a reminder of 50 years since the Stonewall riots. Today she is touring with a recital that she →

ABOVE: Opera singer Jamie Barton performs at the 2019 Last Night of the Proms, held in the Royal Albert Hall, London. She waved the Gay Pride flag there as a reminder it was 50 years since the Stonewall riots

She continued: "On the other side, I have a fabulous base of older, classical music listeners and I've often gotten a lot of positive response from them. A lot of the time it's surprise – surprise that the group of women composers that I have that start the recitals are as breathtaking as they are, because these are composers who maybe they've heard of, or maybe they've even heard some of their music, but they certainly don't know them very well."

Barton describes the response to her recital tour across the USA as "overwhelming", but overwhelming doesn't always mean positive.

"Sometimes it was really negative," she said. "I recall getting messages on Instagram and Twitter – someone wrote at one point: 'Get your bigoted ass out of my town.'

"There's a very loud, and very small, faction of people who were so very much against it. They didn't want me and my progressive values anywhere close to them."

Aware of this, Barton is careful with the words she chooses, and one she avoids when speaking from the stage is "feminist" – not because she has an issue with it (to her it's a "really beautiful word") but because she knows others do.

"I say: 'This is a celebration of women.' There's something about that that becomes more palatable to people of all ages. They get that women don't get celebrated in this form often."

What of working in the age of #metoo? Barton says that she is feeling encouraged, at least within the classical music industry where change is afoot.

"In the last year of my career opera companies have begun to implement sexual harassment training. In my 10 years of doing this professionally on the road, this is the first season that I have known for most opera houses who the HR person is or how to get in touch with them," she said.

Barton hopes that other important conversations will rise up the agenda. This champion of body positivity is incredibly keen to play Carmen but has been overlooked due to her size.

"We've just gotta get the gatekeepers to open their eyes and understand how exclusive, in the negative sense, it is at this point and how beautiful, truthful and powerful it could be if the casting gates were opened a little bit wider," she said.

If anyone can take on the gatekeepers, it's Barton.

→ describes as feminist and gender-bending.

"When I started putting this recital together it was when a lot of political things were happening and, as a woman in particular, I was feeling really downtrodden," she said. "This recital was really born out of the idea of a celebration of women – women composers, women poets, the stories of women – and also toying with gender constructs.

"Really it's just an opportunity to try to challenge the audience to think outside of the normal recital bounds. The fact of the matter is most of the composers, particularly in classical music, are old, dead, white guys so the opportunity to bring in a different perspective is something that really caught me."

Barton says her recitals attract a younger-than-average audience. "With those kinds of crowds it's almost automatically built in that they're really interested in sharing these kinds of things [and they are] very into seeing themselves reflected on stage," she said. This is especially so for women. "They are excited to see and hear something different."

Excited, and emotional too.

"Several would get to me in the receiving line after a recital and would burst into tears, and what they said over and over again was 'Thank you. Thank you, I didn't know this existed, I didn't know there was a place for me in this'."

THE MESSAGE IS IN THE MUSIC

LIDIYA YANKOVSKAYA EMIGRATED with her mum from Russia to the USA in 1995 when she was nine because of the rising tide of anti-Semitism in her home country. But she still maintains fond memories of the music scene there.

The opera singer and composer, who is music director of the Chicago Opera Theater, recently founded the Refugee Orchestra Project. Through this she interacts with people who have not always been granted musical free expression.

"One composer we work with quite a bit is a young man named Milad Yousufi, who now lives in the United States but is originally from Afghanistan," she said. After the fall of the Taliban, when music had been banned, he was one of the first students of music in Afghanistan.

She says that the project promotes togetherness, but adds that "the kind of discord that we are seeing nationwide makes it much more difficult to bring that message of unity and dialogue".

The project has many admirers. A quick look at its Facebook page shows happy concert-goers asking for more, but it has also attracted the occasional message of hate – possibly because of the current tense political climate in the USA.

"When we started the orchestra it wasn't really a political statement to say, 'We are a country of immigrants and a country with a plurality of voices and we'd like to highlight that and celebrate that', but, over the last few years, even reminding people of that has become much more political and elicits a very different response from some individuals," she said.

And as well as musicians from all over the world, she is also working with a large number of composers.

"[They] are combining the traditions that come from the countries where they are from with what they are studying here – with American music, even American popular music – and that's really beautiful, valuable and incredible. That's what moves any art form forward," she said.

"The arts serve such an important role in starting dialogue and bringing people together. Music in particular can start a dialogue in a way that is so relatable to anyone, that is not boxing anyone in, that doesn't have the same connotations or assumptions that language or a visual might presuppose."

Another challenge comes in the form of funding. The US arts funding model is almost wholly reliant on private donors, whose money is often given with certain conditions and expectations attached.

"For the larger arts organisations that means that they are extremely risk averse, that they are afraid to touch more political subject matter out of fear of alienating a donor," said Yankovskaya.

As someone who grew up in a country where the state poured cash into music, she can appreciate what good funding can do.

"In Russia then, and still today, there was so much access to music. One huge positive of the communism era was that music performances were very affordable for people and music education was very widely available.

"I was very fortunate to grow up in this environment because from before I can remember I was regularly going to performances," said Yankovskaya.

Clearly her early music education has stood her in good stead. She might not have left Russia on good terms, but she did leave with good music.

BELOW: Music director and founder of the Refugee Orchestra Project Lidiya Yankovskaya with the orchestra

The final chapter?

A literary landmark in Beijing is being forced to close. **Karoline Kan** explains why one bookshop is incredibly significant

48(04): 64/65 | DOI: 10.1177/0306422019895466

THE BOOKWORM, ONE of the few English bookshops in China and the centre of literary life in Beijing, recently announced it would close after 14 years. The announcement said the closure was not due to operational issues, but it "appears to have fallen prey to the ongoing clean-up of 'illegal structures'," and the owners have not been able to secure an extension of their lease.

"For various reasons I'm keeping a low profile currently and I'm not doing Bookworm interviews," said one of the owners when Index asked about the closure.

The announcement sparked a social media storm among expats and locals. On the bookshop's official page on WeChat – China's Facebook-like social media platform – the announcement was viewed more than 100,000 times (the maximum number the platform would show) within hours. My Twitter feed was also full of comments expressing sadness and surprise.

Why would a bookshop's closing cause such widespread outcry? And what does the closure mean for the exchange of free ideas in the literary community in Beijing?

The Bookworm was more than just a bookshop: it was a library, a bar, a restaurant and an events space. You would be challenged to find another place in China with more freedom of speech than The Bookworm. It was one of the few places in Beijing where you could listen to a panel talk about detained Chinese feminists or hear a North Korean defector's story of escaping her country and finding asylum.

In 14 years it hosted more than 4,000 authors, 12 international literary festivals and numerous fun social events such as quiz nights, poetry readings and films on the rooftop.

It was a place where people with different backgrounds – diplomats, journalists, writers, students and tourists – would meet, talk and make friends.

Tom Baxter, former Beijing Bookworm International Literary Festival programme manager, told Index how sad he felt about the news and highlighted that The Bookworm sold books that were hard to find elsewhere in the city. He said "it was a meeting place where great conversations would begin" and "a source of inspiration for many people".

Located in the central area of Sanlitun, The Bookworm was an oasis in Beijing's ultra urban metropolis, where tradition and history have given way to cement high-rises and shiny, new shopping malls.

It occupied the second floor of a building that used to be an electrical factory but has been renovated into a centre of hipster restaurants, cool nightclubs and bars. The stairs to the bookshop were painted with the names of renowned authors and their books – from George Orwell's Nineteen Eighty-Four to Chinese author Yu Hua's To Live.

I was sad, but not shocked, to see The Bookworm's announcement. Being branded an "illegal structure" has become commonplace for many small businesses in this city. Since 2017, when Beijing started a crackdown on these so-called illegal buildings, many popular venues have been closed down. What the

> *Culture must be state-owned, state-managed and must serve the purpose of the Chinese Communist Party's propaganda. It cannot be grassroots like the culture at The Bookworm*

government wants is a city where every single space, especially those that organise events, is run through central government management.

Culture must be state-owned, state-managed and must serve the purpose of the Chinese Communist Party's propaganda. It cannot be grassroots like the culture at The Bookworm.

Bookshops occupy a special place in many people's lives – especially in China. Censorship and surveillance are prevalent and people need spaces where they can meet in person to discuss any topic without fear of being monitored and reported. But the emergence of e-commerce and digital books, combined with the crackdown on independent spaces, has meant that independent bookshops are dying.

Bookshops have played a really important role in my journey to becoming a writer. I grew up in a small town in northern China where the only thing relevant to literature and culture was a chain bookshop called Xinhua (New China), which was a 15-minute bike ride from my home. In the 1990s and early 2000s, when I was at school, I spent almost every weekend afternoon in that bookshop. It was a place where I could escape into other worlds that weren't all about money, mundane work and gossip.

That 50-square-metre room opened up a world of literature, art, music and dreams to me. Many other Chinese people share similar memories of bookshops, especially those who grew up in small places like I did.

The Bookworm was the place where I saw my dreams come true. Those glorious names printed on the book covers became real – sitting in front of me, talking and laughing with the audience. A few of them even gave me advice. It was at The Bookworm where I met and made friends with other journalists and writers. It was also there where I had romantic evenings with my partner when we first started dating and found we had a lot in common.

Alec Ash shares my views. He launched his book Wish Lanterns there. He told Index: "I feel devastated by the Beijing Bookworm's closure.

The Bookworm has long been a hub for cultural engagement and the free exchange of ideas, both of which are especially important in China today. Bookshops and libraries are a third space that foster free speech, and I hope that that space will not shrink too much further without it."

The Bookworm is trying to relocate somewhere else, so it's too early to say if this is its own final chapter. But can it ever be what it was? Anthony Tao, editor at digital magazine SupChina and Bookworm quiz night organiser, thinks not.

"It won't be the same because of the institutional memory in the old location. That's real, because real people – thousands upon thousands – were there, at that spot, when memorable things happened."

At the last quiz night there, everyone cheered for the great memories it had provided and wished it good luck relocating. People need bookshops, and they need them more than ever today as an antidote to our retreat online. Face-to-face debating, the sympathy gained from offline communications and the sense of security and freedom from a warm and welcoming place are hard to come by. I hope it's not "goodbye", just "see you soon". ⊗

Karoline Kan *is a regular contributor to Index. She is based in Beijing*

ABOVE: Karoline Kan (top right) speaks at The Bookworm, a legendary bookshop and venue in Beijing, that is now closing down

Working it out

Steven Borowiec talks to **Park Chang-jin,** the airline steward who famously was forced to kneel by an angry South Korean passenger, about workplace bullying and if it has improved

48(04): 66/68 I DOI: 10.1177/0306422019895467

GROUND ZERO OF the current movement to eliminate workplace bullying in South Korea is a cramped 10th-floor office in central Seoul, where the four members of staff watch their email inboxes constantly fill with cries for help. Gabjill119 was formed in 2017 to provide victims of workplace bullying with guidance on how they could fight back, and to gather facts on the extent of the problem in the country's hierarchical offices, factories, restaurants and farms.

And the problem is huge. Workplace bullying has been at the core of South Korea's public discourse since 2014, after Cho Hyun-ah, a member of the family that owns flagship airline Korean Air, berated a flight attendant for serving her macadamia nuts in an unopened bag instead of on a plate.

Cho reportedly commanded the purser, Park Chang-jin, to kneel in apology and ordered the plane, at JFK airport in New York, to return to the terminal so she could kick Park off the flight.

That incident made headlines around the world and, in South Korea, sparked a national conversation on entitled and callous behaviour by the rich and powerful elite. Since then, that discourse has evolved to include interactions involving people who may not be rich or powerful but who do use some kind of leverage to demean others.

Park has led public campaigns to rid South Korean workplaces of the kind of treatment he experienced. "We are told just to endure and, if we get attacked, just keep quiet. To change things, we need to get together and acknowledge that so many people suffer like I did, and that should change," he told Index.

"In Korean society employees are told to just follow the rules and don't disobey, then you'll get a salary. Most people think like that. And my co-workers also think that I should be in awe of my boss, and not draw attention to these shameful things. Even though we have a problem, most people tell me, don't reveal it to other people.

"Korean people think, even though you were attacked, or you were a victim, you should keep quiet, don't insist on your own gain. If you do that you are not pure any more.

"In some way, our country is like North Korea, in that only a few people have all the power and they ask other people to sacrifice, without caring much about human rights."

Analysts say bullying has been a feature of Korean organisations going back at least to the early 20th century, when the country was occupied by the Japanese empire. "Korea's whole experience of modernisation was forced. It came from being under a military occupation, then after independence under a series of military dictatorships," said Michael Hurt, a research professor at the University of Seoul.

"Everything is still organised under military-style hierarchies, where everyone is either under someone else's thumb or trying to keep people under their own thumb."

In one infamous case, video footage of Yang Jin-ho, a tech CEO, brutally assaulting an employee circulated online. The video was taken by many as evidence that it isn't only old-fashioned corporate workplaces where the worst kinds of bullying take place.

Another incident made national headlines when local media reported that a hospital forced nurses to don revealing outfits and perform a provocative, K-pop style dance routine as part of an annual company gathering.

We are told just to endure and, if we get attacked, just keep quiet

In this environment, the work of Gabjil119 is essential. The organisation is named because 119 is the Korean equivalent of 911 or 999, the emergency phone number, and "*gabjil*" is a Korean word that refers to older or more powerful people using their status to bully or intimidate those they see as beneath them.

Gabjil119 does not intervene in workplace disputes and has no mandate to advocate directly for workers in disputes with employers.

The group's main task is to educate workers on the law – specifically, what their employers can legally make them do and how workers can push back if an employer violates the law.

There is pent-up demand for their services. *Gabjil* is a big enough deal in South Korea that the president has declared changing the culture of bullying to be an official policy goal. A recent survey released by the South Korean legislature showed that 77% of workers at →

Gabjil is a big enough deal in South Korea that the president has declared changing the culture of bullying to be an official policy goal

→ one government body were not aware of any way to deal with workplace bullying other than to simply endure it.

The group is also out to change what members see as shortcomings in labour law. The first major success came in the summer of 2018 with the passage of legislation that required South Korean companies to investigate allegations of bullying. Under the law, companies found to have unfairly demoted or fired workers who have spoken out about having been harassed at work are subject to punishment.

The staff at Gabjil119 celebrated the passage of the law, but they feel the legislation doesn't go far enough, as it doesn't mandate punishment for bullies – only for companies that fail to investigate complaints of bullying or reprimand perpetrators. Even if a company's internal investigation concludes that a boss has mistreated an employee, the company is under no legal obligation to take action.

Park Jum-kyu, a co-founder of Gabjil119, said: "The work environment is changing in terms of how people interact, but when it comes to things involving money, like workers not getting paid or being forced to do unpaid overtime, that hasn't changed."

Park said: "People are scared that if they call attention to bullying there could be consequences, like they could be pushed out of the company or their colleagues will turn against them."

In October, a few months after the law's passage, Gabjil119 released the results of a survey of 1,000 working people, asking if conditions in workplaces had changed since the legislation came into effect. The results showed that 40% answered that things had changed for the better, and 80% said they would like the scope of the law to be expanded, with punishments for perpetrators.

Park says the data indicates that young workers are still vulnerable. "It's mostly people in their 40s and 50s that think that the culture is changing. They're at the age of most perpetrators of *gabjil*, and they're scared of the law and they feel like they need to be more careful. But young people feel like things haven't really changed," he said.

To connect with mobile-savvy young people, Gabjil119 operates a chatroom on Kakao, South Korea's most-used mobile messaging service (think WhatsApp with a more alluring colour scheme and cuter emojis). Throughout the day, the chatroom swells with hundreds of messages, as working people reach out for advice. Gabjil119 staff members take turns moderating the chat, responding to each claim and sorting claimants into separate chatrooms which are specialised for workers in particular industries, including call centres, childcare and healthcare.

As its next major objective, Gabjil119 is lobbying the government to phase out South Korea's widespread and growing use of dispatch and contract employment, which can leave workers more vulnerable to mistreatment or lost wages, and make people afraid to speak out. The group also liaises with workers to discuss creating industry-specific unions that would allow workers to collectively bargain with employers.

Alex Taek-Gwang Lee, a professor at the Kyung Hee University School of Global Communication in Seoul, said: "*Gabjil* is an outcome of this society's polarisation – the fact that it's 10% of the country that runs the whole place. The term *gabjil* itself has limits, in that it describes relations between two particular parties and doesn't factor in the fundamental structure of society.

"But Korean society is keen on the building of consensus. These kinds of campaigns can push the perception of *gabjil* to the surface and spur policy changes." ⊗

Steven Borowiec *is a regular correspondent for Index on Censorship based in Seoul, South Korea*

Protest works

The news is often full of unsuccessful stories of protest. **Rachael Jolley** and **Jemimah Steinfeld** talk to two activists whose innovative approaches have actually affected real change

48(04): 69/72 | DOI: 10.1177/0306422019895468

THE POWER OF SILENCE

With a new Romanian government just sworn in, writer Radu Vancu tells RACHAEL JOLLEY that he wants to inform the world that protests have the power to change everything

POET, ACADEMIC AND editor Radu Vancu is feeling hopeful that two years of protests in Romania are about to result in significant and positive change for his country.

Vancu, who is the spokesman for the protesters, as well as one of the organisers, said: "It's rather surprising for us in Romania that this, our protest story, is a success story because we started in a state of complete hopelessness."

When people around the world talk about protests not working, or giving up on freedom of expression because it doesn't seem important, then my advice is to sit down with Vancu and listen to why he thinks differently.

As Index goes to press, the two years of weekly silent protests are on hold: Romania has a new government and the protest movement is giving it a chance to make good on its promises. The protesters have called on this new government to make sure every Romanian gets a vote (there were recent elections when people had to wait 12 hours to do just that); to re-establish the rule of law without loopholes relating to corruption; and to make sure mayoral elections are run fairly.

With Prime Minister Ludovic Orban sworn in at the beginning of November, Romanian activists are waiting hopefully. Right now, they believe their protests caused the last government to fall and that widespread public action is about to produce historic changes in Romania's parliamentary democracy.

"If you protest long enough you win, actually," said Vancu. "For me it is obvious. It creates a community of memory and of feeling."

The protests started when a previous government, led by the Social Democratic (PSD) party, tried to introduce a law that would have protected politicians from being prosecuted for corruption of public funds for sums less than €200,000 ($220,361).

From January 2017, thousands of people massed outside to show their anger. On 1 February, the day after the new law was brought in, people poured onto the streets. An estimated 300,000 demonstrated that day, rising to 500,000 later in the month.

Vancu said: "We had witnessed how corruption is not something abstract, but something that has impact on some of the most concrete levels of life – on education, on healthcare systems, on emergency systems and so on. We felt that if the last fortress standing, that of the rule of law,

is destroyed by corruption, then Romania is a failed state.

"So this was outrageous. We got out into the streets, we started fighting with them – they had shown us that they intended to do even more, to decriminalise some other dozens of corruption deeds in order to get all the politicians free of the consequences of their illegal facts.

"We reacted with despair, with hopelessness, with rage against this attempt to help the leader of [the] so-called social democrat party to be exempt from the punishments of corruption."

It worked by bringing together all sorts of people from all sorts of backgrounds to work together – and by the fact that they kept going, week after week.

"We knew that we had to be effective in order to beat them," said Vancu. "Being effective meant drawing in as many social classes, as many people, as many levels of education, ages, and so on, in order not to have only a middle-class protest but in order to have a protest unifying all people in Romania who felt that the country was going in the wrong direction."

Once the alliance was created, they also looked at the tactics of being heard and being influential.

"It was really important for us to get the international press interested in us," said Vancu. "We had support from important newspapers and televisions in the US, in the European area, and this really put pressure on the politicians because they don't like to see their faces exposed there."

International bodies including the US government and embassies from Germany, France and Canada began to speak out against the change in legislation.

Then the Romanian politicians decided to try to silence the protesters and their critics.

"They even tried to create a defamation law to forbid us to talk to the foreign press," said Vancu. "It was a project which they eventually abandoned due to international press protests because European institutions said, 'OK, you are a European country, you have a constitution stipulating the right to free expression so you should let people talk'.

"[The government] tried to make both normal citizens like me and European politicians coming from Romania in the European parliament shut up, and otherwise be imprisoned or taken from their positions."

In the first few weeks there was no need to organise the protests: people were so fired up that they poured out onto the streets. But then, admits Vancu, they were hit by tiredness and they knew they needed a new approach. They decided to use a new, slower tactic.

"We announced we would come every day at noon in front of the PSD headquarters and stay there,

ABOVE: Romanian activist Radu Vancu, who took part in two years of silent protest

CREDIT: (left) Rachael Jolley/Index on Censorship; (top) Alberto Grosescu/Alamy; (right) Zsofia Borcsök

LEFT: A chair abandoned after a protest in Bucharest, Romania in 2018

create a network of silent protests in Romania, hopefully in all cities, because we thought, 'it is simple, easy to organise, with a minimum of discussing the situation'."

As well as the silent protests they organised discussions, which drew huge audiences online, where people would debate what could happen next.

And he has a message for those who think the rule of law and freedom of expression are not worth fighting for.

"The thing is, we don't see the results immediately. We live in an age where we are used to pushing a button on a phone and seeing the immediate results ... you protest now, and maybe in two years you will see the results. It is a long time for people – it is difficult to keep doing it."

It might be contrary to the instant gratification we are used to but, in the end, he said: "You have a voice, and you have power, you regain your self esteem. You feel determination once again."

Rachael Jolley is the editor-in-chief of Index on Censorship

silent, and watch them, watch the windows of the party, in order to show them that we see them, and we wanted it to be silent because we found it powerful symbolically," he said.

"If you keep silent they cannot manipulate silence: silence is pure, is clean, is effective, and we thought a silent protest would speak even louder."

It did, and Vancu added: "We hoped this would

MARSHALLING ORBAN'S OPPOSITION

Budapest has a new mayor. JEMIMAH STEINFELD talks to activist Dóra Papp about how she helped get him elected despite pushback from the government

HUNGARIAN ACTIVIST DÓRA Papp told Index that when it came to free expression in her country there was no "space for it to worsen". Faced with that challenge, she had to get creative. As a founder of the new grassroots organisation aHang (The Voice) – whose mission statement is to take action regarding important public issues and provide new ways and means to effect change – Papp and those in her network mix innovative online approaches to campaigning with old school, get out onto the streets and talk to people styles. And they've managed to challenge the ruling Fidesz Party as a result.

Part of the success of their community strategy is that they don't just talk to people, they listen.

"When aHang start a petition, it means we also survey people. If people are not reacting, the signatures are not high enough, that topic is basically not ready yet to take off," said Papp.

When Papp says "take off", she is not mincing her words. Earlier this year they were contacted by the opposition politician Gergely Karácsony about the

possibility of helping him organise the local governmental primary elections. The idea behind it was to coordinate the campaign – in order to challenge a rigged political system, a united opposition was key.

They weren't sure whether they should get involved until they sent out a questionnaire, which approximately 2,000 people completed.

The majority supported their decision. In part as a result of aHang's canvassing – which involved teaming up with 40 other organisations, a viral online campaign and hundreds of volunteers getting out onto the streets – Karácsony won the mayoral election in Budapest this October, ousting the ruling party incumbent.

The opposition also won a number of other Hungarian cities. This became the first major defeat for Fidesz in an election since 2006 – and the first time a civil organisation has organised a primary election in Hungary.

"Access to information as well as disinformation is a huge (and still growing) problem in Hungary", she told Index.

"You have to find ways of shouting over the barricades," she said.

The barricades really are as high as she says. In Hungary, independent media has almost disappeared and the main outlets are owned by government allies, university courses and academics are suffering (the Central European University had to relocate to Vienna last month), the arts are under attack – all the normal avenues of communicating →

LEFT: Activist Dóra Papp, whose organisation helped elect opposition candidates in recent elections in Hungary

and migrants are also at the receiving end of ill treatment, with Orbán describing them as "poison".

And Papp adds that this marginalisation extends to women.

"Women should be mothers and bear children. They should be part of this brainless framework. It's Desperate Housewives: the Fidesz version," she said.

But the very people who should be out voting, or having their voices heard in other ways, are often not. This was evident in 2016, when less than half the voting population turned out for a referendum on whether Hungary should close its doors to refugees. It had one positive – with such a small turnout the result was declared null and void.

Had more people turned out it could have been very different. As it stood, 98% of voters sided with Orbán and, even though the vote was not legally binding, he saw it as a personal victory. Where were the voices of those who did not side with him?

aHang took on low voter turnout within Roma communities ahead of the 2018 general elections. They teamed up with Roma celebrities and made a series of videos as part of a campaign to call on people to vote. They wanted to talk to them directly, and in a way that they could relate to. Papp said that many people within the community had never voted and did not know there were other options beyond Fidesz.

Of course not all are receptive to the more personal approach, which Papp acknowledges. And yet even when the response might appear frosty, the result can be positive. This year, for example, aHang activists, together with members of the public, managed to pressure the National Roma Self-Government to reinstall a memorial plaque which commemorated six Roma who were murdered in 2009.

They did this through a multi-pronged strategy which involved continuously knocking on the door of the local government. The door never opened and so they decided to cover it with their messages. Without any acknowledgement, the plaque was reinstalled.

It's all about getting people to identify a case in whichever way is best, says Papp, who also works in the arts and tells Index about the value of "feeling your audience".

The real test will come in 2022, when Hungarians go to the polls for their next general elections. With two years to go, can they talk to enough people to help fully change the tide of politics in Hungary?

Jemimah Steinfeld is deputy editor of Index

→ information and challenging governmental power are basically cut off.

"If you're not silent then we don't have room for you," is the message of the ruling party Fidesz, according to Papp, who said: "The only enemy in this system is the dissident who is open about their opinion, which is confronting the government."

But people want to talk.

"People are really eager to be interviewed. They want to take part. Asking people what their needs are is really important," she said.

Of course this can happen online, and aHang primarily use modern technology, but there is something about getting away from the screen and meeting people that is particularly effective.

"You get a connection with them," Papp said.

The personal approach is desperately needed in Hungary. Fidesz and its leader, Prime Minister Viktor Orbán, expound a right-wing traditional form of politics which, as Papp says, has seen the country's marginalised being attacked.

Hungary's Roma population is particularly singled out for ill treatment.

In 2013, one of the founders of Fidesz, Zsolt Bayer, called the Roma "animals ... unfit to live among people" and the party turns a blind eye to the hate crimes that the Roma experience on a day to day basis. Refugees

It's a little bit silent, this feeling inside

Taboos surrounding suicide still exist in Spain and prevent people from talking about it, writes
Silvia Nortes

48(04): 73/75 I DOI: 10.1177/0306422019895469

"**IT WILL BE** very difficult to talk with someone who has survived suicide," said María Guerrero, regional president of Teléfono de la Esperanza (Phone of Hope), an NGO that provides qualified help to anyone having suicidal thoughts.

Guerrero's words reflect the patina of rejection and shame that still covers the treatment of suicide in Spain.

According to data from the National Statistics Institute (INE), 3,679 people took their own lives in 2017. That figure – the highest in the last 12 years – means that an average of 10 people die by suicide every day in Spain. And there might be many more.

Javier Jiménez, a clinical psychologist and member of the Asociación de Investigación, Prevención e Intervención del Suicido Network, which works to prevent suicides, told Index: "There are about 8,000 accidental deaths in Spain every year and it is very difficult to prove which of them are suicides. Many suicides are registered by the Judicial Commission as accidents, such as 'accidental drug intake' or 'accidental fall', because there is neither a farewell note nor a witness to confirm them."

Suicide is the main reason for deaths in Spain which are not the result of disease, double the number caused by traffic accidents.

Next year will mark the end of the World Health Organisation's mental health action plan 2013-2020, which saw member states committing themselves to work towards reducing suicide rates by 10%. However, in Spain, suicide remains not only a social taboo but a political, media and educational one, too.

The origin can be found in Spain's religious heritage. As Jiménez said: "For 1,500 years, both the victims and their families have been severely punished. Until 1984, a person who had committed suicide could not be buried in a Christian cemetery."

Families hid suicides so as not to be marked by the stigma of sin, and the tradition has evolved into what Susana al-Halabí, professor of the department of psychology at the University of Oviedo, calls the current "philosophy of happiness", which "generates a breeding ground for hopelessness".

According to al-Halabí: "In the era of social media and feigned happiness, those suffering feel abandoned: lacking a space to express themselves to have their suffering validated by others."

The social taboo is also reflected in media coverage.

Coral Larrosa is vice-president of the National Association of Health Reporters and a health journalist for TV channel Telecinco. "There has always been kind of a tacit agreement whereby suicides were not reported to avoid imitation," she said.

This refers to the so-called Werther effect, the imitative effect of suicidal behaviour. On the other side is the Papageno effect, which says that good information related to suicide may have a preventive effect.

→

There is a myth that if a person talks about suicide, the chances of carrying it through might increase. On the contrary, it creates an opportunity for that person to ask for help

The number of victims of traffic accidents has been greatly reduced since communication campaigns have been carried out, and the same can be achieved for suicide

→ International bodies such as the WHO, which states that "responsible reporting of suicide in the media has been shown to be effective in limiting imitation among vulnerable people", and The Lancet Psychiatry journal are trying to reverse the trend of ignoring suicides.

Larrosa says that outlets are now being told that not reporting suicides does nothing to discourage others, adding: "We have to report not only on the event itself but on mental health, while giving tools to people who may be going through it."

To this end, guidelines for suicide coverage have been published recently. Recommendations from the Mental Health Observatory include avoiding describing the method used and highlighting information on where to seek help.

The WHO also offers resources for media professionals, but this document has not been translated into Spanish and it is up to local or regional associations to adapt these guidelines.

Larrosa feels this puts a lot of responsibility on the media. "We are not health or justice workers. The administration cannot leave its responsibility of reaching society in the hands of the media," she said.

There are many apparent deficiencies in the treatment of suicidal behaviour in the country.

First, there is no prevention plan at a national level, despite legislative initiatives such as the motion promoted in 2017 by the Unión del Pueblo Navarro party, which called for a national suicide prevention plan.

The motion was approved by Congress, but the resignation of Carmen Montón, the then minister of health, paralysed the process.

Even universities fail to adequately talk about suicide. There is no suicide treatment and prevention course at any of the 29 Spanish psychology faculties, with only Seville's Pablo de Olavide University offering an online master's degree in suicide prevention. The Acting Against Suicide workshop at the Universidad Autónoma de Madrid and the summer course in prevention and intervention in suicidal behaviour at the University of Castilla-La Mancha are the only others on offer.

Independently, the Spanish Foundation for the Prevention of Suicide has launched the Institute of Training in Suicidology.

"Thousands of psychologists are graduating every year without preparation in this area," said Jiménez. "We must teach how to detect, intervene and treat suicidal behaviour."

In response to this educational gap, psychologist Aminta Pedrosa decided to contact all faculties of psychology, medicine, nursing, social work and occupational therapy with a proposal to include training in suicidal and self-harming behaviour in their curriculum. Only five faculties showed interest.

"Everything is left to the personal initiative of professors who decide to talk about suicide," Pedrosa said.

And this is not easy, because the taboo exists also among professionals, who are cautious of tackling the issues with their patients for fear of exacerbating them.

As a consequence, care for those affected is largely in the hands of independent non-profit associations.

"At AIPIS, we are totally overwhelmed – even people from South America write to us," said Jiménez.

In addition to the lack of human resources, there is no public funding. "Not only do we not receive financial support, we are not given any premises for, for example, training activities."

But some regional governments and independent groups are mobilising to try to help solve the problem.

In the Extremadura region, a protocol to detect suicidal behaviour is being implemented in 2020. The Balearic Islands' government is promoting a protocol to prevent suicide in schools and, in Catalonia, the Codi Risc Suïcidi (Suicide Risk Code) programme has been

working since 2014, ensuring a homogeneous response by emergency services.

So how can suicide figures be reduced? Breaking the taboo through communication seems essential. As Pedrosa says: "The number of victims of traffic accidents has been greatly reduced since communication campaigns have been carried out, and the same can be achieved for suicide."

Al-Halabí highlights the "emotional ventilation" generated by talking about suicide.

"Sharing those thoughts is a great relief for people who suffer them," she said. "There is a myth that if a person talks about suicide, the chances of carrying it through might increase. On the contrary, it creates an opportunity for that person to ask for help." ✖

Silvia Nortes is a freelance journalist based in Murcia, Spain

Contact AIPIS for help on www.redaipis.org

PICTURED: An anti-government protester reacts to police tear gas during a march in Hong Kong

CULTURE

78 HONG KONG WRITES TAMMY LAI-MING HO
Tammy Lai-Ming Ho tells **Jemimah Steinfeld**
how she is using poetry to show solidarity
with those protesting in Hong Kong. We
publish one of her poems for the first time

80 WRITING TO THE CHALLENGE KAYA GENÇ
Orna Herr introduces an exclusive short story
by Turkish author **Kaya Genç** that examines
the use of allegory to combat censorship

86 PLAYING THE JOKER JONATHAN TEL
Rachael Jolley speaks to writer **Jonathan
Tel** about the power of joke telling and
introduces his new short story

94 GOING GRAPHIC ANDALUSIA KNOLL
SOLOFF & MARCO PARRA
Andalusia Knoll Soloff tells **Jessica Ní
Mhainín** how graphic novels can be a great
form of communication. We publish her
graphic novelette, artwork by **Marco Parra**

Hong Kong writes

Jemimah Steinfeld speaks to **Tammy Lai-Ming Ho** about how she stands up for Hong Kong rights through poetry

48(04): 78/79 | DOI: 10.1177/0306422019894892

LEFT: Poet Tammy Lai-Ming Ho

HONG KONG RESIDENT Tammy Lai-Ming Ho wears many hats – editor, translator, professor – but her most important hat right now is that of poet.

"We call the current movement the water movement," the award-winning poet tells Index as she talks about the protests that have eclipsed Hong Kong since June.

"We don't have leaders, and people are doing different things. They compose songs, they design posters, they play music, they come up with slogans, they create new Chinese [written] characters," Ho said, adding that she encourages people to write poetry as another contribution.

And she practises what she preaches. Ho has written prolifically on the protests since their inception, saying: "The most direct thing I can do is use poetry to react to a specific day or theme or image."

The most direct thing I can do is use poetry to react to a specific day or theme or image

Her poems, including the one published here for the first time, mix tones of anger with defiance.

"Poetry can serve as a documentation of Hong Kong's current protests in a way that is different from straightforward journalistic pieces, or even photographs," she said. "It has a space for imagination… We are responding to events or images that speak to us."

Ho says that each day can see her emotions jump from hope to despair. When we speak, she is upset.

"It seems we're heading towards a more violent place, and also [one] with a lot of mistrust between different people in the city, who all actually want Hong Kong to be better," she said. She says there has been an increase in police brutality, and mentions a student who fell from a high building while trying to get away from tear gas, who has since died.

And she says that whether you are for them or against them, the protests are difficult to avoid.

"There are so many different things going on. In Hong Kong this is very unusual and unprecedented," she said, acknowledging that Hong Kong was not a stranger to protest, but that the length of these current protests made them stand out. To

guarantee their future success, she believes that "consistency and constancy" will be key.

"We need to be very patient, to continue to go out, and to not stop," she said.

"[We] also need to have the help and assistance of foreign media to not have our story silenced or marginalised – to have our story told to the rest of the world."

Is there anything that she wouldn't write about for fear of repercussions? Despite warnings from many people close to her to be careful, she is keen to avoid censoring herself. But there is one topic that is off-limits – her family.

"Even though my own family members don't read English, they can still use Google Translate. I don't want to cause disharmony in the family," Ho said, explaining that they did not all share the same political views.

As for those living across the border, she is not sure whether her work is being read by people in mainland China – many of whom are only hearing about the protests through a heavily-censored and biased media. Would she like her poems to be read there? She answers instantly, enthusiastically. "Yes, I would love that."

Jemimah Steinfeld *is deputy editor of Index on Censorship magazine*

OPPOSITE: A protester at Yuen Long, Hong Kong, faces riot police

A people of heightened determination

by Tammy Lai-Ming Ho

Protesters wear masks
only because being unmasked is risky,
opening up their faces to a city
of swallowing smoke, toxic,
the background of a dystopian movie –
Several shades more horrible.

No one would choose
to be dehumanised, called cockroaches,
expressions robbed. Legs running
from the first sound of batons. The streets
are streets of wounds and interrogation,
of blood and imagination,
of ripped families, of names that are yelled
when voices are brutally lifted.

Now, put those faces of torture away
and only then speak of unmasking protesters.
They have long discovered
who's selling this city, who's making it rot
from the very, very top. So-called 'public interest'
for these agents of power is but one block
in a child's toy box.

We want to breathe the air of freedom –
people are treated like humans, not pieces of bone
to be picked or raw meat beaten to tender.
Long succession of nights
has birthed a people of heightened determination.
Watch, whenever there's a reason,
we will be fighting. We are fighting.

....

Tammy Lai-Ming Ho *is a writer, translator and editor. She teaches at Hong Kong Baptist University*

Writing to the challenge

Orna Herr talks to Turkish author **Kaya Genç** about hiding hard truths behind soft words

48(04): 80/85 I DOI: 10.1177/0306422019894893

LEFT: Turkish writer Kaya Genç, who believes writers have a duty to challenge censorship

"**ALLEGORY IS A** last resort for Turkish writers" is Kaya Genç's summary of how writers deal with the ongoing assault on freedom of expression in Turkey. Genç's short story, A Piece of Hay, which has been written exclusively for this magazine, demonstrates how script-writers are having to disguise messages by using allegory. People like to see their lives reflected on television, but censorship is making that hard and forcing writers to get creative.

"They cannot show political dissent or sexual relations or any of these anti-hero characters. So, what is the solution?" Genç said in an interview with Index.

A Piece of Hay follows the writing

There is a huge readership for fiction and it means people take your writing seriously, so if you want to make a point people will think about it

team of a show on Turkflix, a fictional streaming service. Upon the president's insistence that Turkish morality must be protected, the team masks sexual storylines with innocuous words and images – a process which also happens in real life.

"Writers are alarmed because there are big budgets in these shows, so they have to change certain things so that they are not banned from air," he said. "They have to be complicit in this kind of censorship."

Asked if he had been inspired by the work of George Orwell, he said: "There is a Stalinist trend in Turkey. It's like becoming a party state. There are people trying to serve that party state and show their alliance to the leader, so if they want to complain about power, or the political system, they can't put it in a realistic frame because they're concerned that they will be cancelled. There is that kind of Orwellian layer to what's going on now."

He says novelists are just as challenged by the censors, who take fiction very seriously – whether on television or in a book.

"If one of your characters says something politically problematic, the prosecutor can come after you," said Genç, who has direct experience of this from when he was 23.

"I wrote a short story in a fiction magazine and someone complained," he said.

He was accused of having the same views as his character and had to go to the prosecutor, taking his father along because he was concerned and wanted to make a good impression.

"I remember there was a typist, she was typing whatever I said – that irony means this and allegory means that – because I was trying to get rid of this kind of allegation and then I think he [the prosecutor] believed me and he said: 'You're a good boy. I'm going to deal with other things'."

Genç believes it is crucial that fiction writers continue to challenge the censors, saying: "There is a huge readership for fiction and it means people take your writing seriously, so if you want to make a point people will think about it."

"You can really show people that freedom of expression is under attack. It makes fiction writing in Turkey exciting because you are trying to avoid pitfalls, and you have this sense of mission. It's a difficult balance but it also makes it worth trying."

While novelists are still using their real names, Turkish website sourtimes.org allows people to freely discuss politics using disguised avatars. But Genç believes this anonymity holds people back.

"Everyone thinks they're rebels. 'We are writing on this website; we are actually rebelling against the government'. But you don't know who they are. The government succeeds in locking you up in your anonymity.

So, as a political force, you cannot emerge on the public scene."

The message Genç wants to leave his readers with is that representing reality is a privilege that should not be taken for granted.

"European art is built on realism and it is something we have to fight for because it's not just an art concept: it's a way of looking at life, and it can be taken away from us very easily."

Genç, who recently released The Lion and the Nightingale: A Journey Through Modern Turkey, in which he talks about the gap between our public and private selves, added: "I think what censorship does to us is to widen that gap." ⊗

Orna Herr *is the editorial assistant at Index on Censorship*

A piece of hay

By Kaya Genç

THE CONFERENCE ROOM is equipped with chairs, charging docks and bottled water from the Swiss Alps. Its dark walls glow as a bespectacled girl, a burly man and a writer, dressed in suits, enter the room in single file.

"These automated lights," says the writer, "threaten our agency. I'd much prefer a manual conference room." They are here to finalise the script of the new episode of The Empire of Love, their Turkflix show about two women's rivalry to win the heart of one Bearded Son of a Turkish Tycoon.

For three seasons things went smoothly for their show: millions of views, fat ad revenue from chocolate and condom makers, and a flurry of interest from the press. But last night's breaking news complicated this afternoon's work.

On Twitter, the President pledged to "put a leash" on streaming services, like Turkflix, "in order to defend our innocent boys and girls". The instruction from Turkflix HQ, hastily issued soon afterwards, ordered the producer to "tame" their show and make it compatible with "Turkish morality".

But the Turkish producer isn't sure what Turkish morality means. "We'll need to be careful, closeted, a bit muted," he tells his team, though he doesn't know how. "Jane Austen, Henry James, those Edwardian, Victorian double-dealers. Like them we'll be all innuendo and little action. We'll cater to our President's old-fashioned tastes. We'll be decent and pure. We'll be subtle by law. This is surely a challenge, but it may also be fun."

But the cliffhanger of last season's finale was a suspended threesome, and the challenge may be too large to overcome. In that scene Ambitious Banker and Barista Poet laid on Rich Boy's thighs, wearing robes, and eyeing the camera as it panned between their conniving faces. For sponsors the scene was full of financial promise. The Empire of Love's media coverage largely comprised photo galleries of lingerie worn in such occasions. Without erotica their revenue would dry.   →

→ Now the writer says she can't believe their misfortune. "This is a ruthless assault on our agency! First the government came for cigarettes. We didn't speak out because our characters take ecstasy instead. Then they came for alcohol. We didn't speak out because Rich Boy prefers gambling. They came for swearwords and we didn't speak out because Ambitious Banker and Barista Poet plot each other's downfall using posh language. Now the state comes for what it calls elitism, and there is no one left to speak for us."

The President had accused subscription-based "elitist" streaming services of affronting "Turkey's purity". Affluent Turks, he claimed, "believe they are subject to different rules", and he urged his followers to "teach them a lesson."

Who could argue with him? Nobody has the power. The writer paces the conference room anxiously, play-acting victimhood – a character from a court drama. "As a nation," she says, "we scrutinise by punches and make up by blowjobs. Now censors ask us to tame those emotions. Our characters, in their view, should behave civilly and talk articulately. And I tell this to censors: they can't, and they won't! Would characters in Goodfellas behave like characters in The Age of Innocence? I ask you to ponder the question for a moment and find a way to fix this disaster." The bespectacled girl notes the titles; the meeting is adjourned.

That afternoon she buys a copy of Edith Wharton's novel from the bookstore adjacent to Starbucks. She hopes that will solve the crisis. It doesn't. While eating her lentils, Wharton's prose remains unfathomable. She packs the book, switches to Wikipedia, texts her boss ("Ambiguity, complexity: can we turn this into an advantage?") but spends the next ten minutes poring over her notebook. She scribbles, crosses out and flips back: lengthy depictions of her dreams from last August strike her with their awful imagery. But they also intrigue her. They are uncensored, raw and absurd.

Meanwhile the producer is busy reading Lucky Luke upstairs, and he ignores his phone. As a kid he was introduced to Luke by that iconic cigarette. When a piece of hay replaced it in 1983, he was saddened. When the same happened to Sanji, a hero of the Japanese comics One Piece, and a lollipop substituted the pirate-cum-cook-cum-cart-vendor's cigarette, he was confused. Why did things need to change? Now he knows what forces them to change. This is a test, he knows, and he has to prove his leadership by steering his team away from troubled waters.

That evening he sits down with his assistant. They pore over her notebook. On a new page they list problematic content – premarital sex, adultery, violence, alcoholic beverages, political commentary, threesomes – and ponder possible replacements: raccoons, fireworks, swords, and the Sea Moss Cocktail, a Caribbean beverage made from milk and seaweed.

She comes up with the scheme; they are her dream images; she tells him how her mother first advised her to keep a dream diary. He cherishes his good luck and her troubled dreams. "He plays with his raccoon," she says an hour later with an atomic physicist's seriousness. "She will have fireworks, and she will fondle them," he says. They sketch the continuation of the suspended scene on the next page. "He will now have a sword in his hand, and her finger will rest on its edge," →

THE EMPIRE OF LOVE

@badiuco

ONLY ON
TURKFLIX

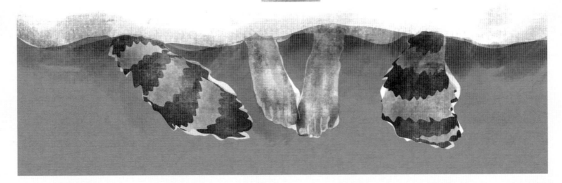

→ she says. "Meanwhile he will wolf a Sea Moss Cocktail," they say in unison.

This is how it'll work. They will compile and release more of these "replacement images" on the dark web, hoping that viewers – millennials well-versed in cheat codes and other features of gaming culture – will engage viscerally with their cryptic dream-like content. They will figure out what the show makers want to say but can't. Their show will be the nation's subconscious.

First actors will get it. Like teenagers, they'll conceal and insinuate, imply and wink. Once they get it, viewers will get it, too. "The headmaster is in class; let's talk in codes." "Oh, but that scene was just a dream." This is the language of oppressed childhood for Turks: the god-like image of Ataturk inspecting them in classrooms as they guiltily invent phrases for self-expression. This will strike a chord and catch the government off-guard.

Not everyone will like it. Of course not. "What a stupid idea," the writer says the next day. "If doublespeak is your solution to censorship, we are doomed. How can we claim to represent reality with these secret 'replacement images'? They're an automated solution to an elaborate problem. Besides, they take away our agency!"

People are hooked. Ambitious Banker and Barista Poet feed raccoons, and people find it hilarious, and they watch the scene over and over again

---

But three weeks later she'll be drinking champagne from the producer's Rolexed hand, sitting half-drunk on the conference room table, wearing Jimmy Choos. And she will say sorry. "I was mistaken." The trick has worked. #Raccoon has been trending on Turkish Twitter; firework emojis have dominated sexts. A government adviser has warned against "those who want sword on our streets" while condemning activism. "You were involved in fireworks when your family needed you" a judge has told an adulterer before giving his wife their kid's custody.

By the end of the year, they had reached dry land. Ad revenue quadrupled. Covers belonged to them, as did talk show sofas. Rich Boy became an icon, despite lines like "the anchovy flattens Apollo 13". "The anchovy" is "my heart"; "flatten" is "desire"; "Apollo 13" is "Barista Poet's lips". Turkish morality is saved, and Turkish purity conserved. Gossip columnists say even the President binges on their show these days; the rumour is that he keeps a Sea Moss Cocktail next to his desk.

*

Now begins work for the final season, but there are changes. The assistant no longer wears glasses. She confesses to finding the Victorianism of their product "out of control", "dangerously erotic". She is in a bad mood. Alarmed, anxious, apathetic. She wants out.

But it isn't easy. People are hooked. Ambitious Banker and Barista Poet feed raccoons, and people find it hilarious, and they watch the scene over and over again. Rich Boy tastes an almond, and there is applause, and he is a trending topic. His father, the Tycoon, talks about a panda, and laughter arises from Turkish living rooms and WhatsApp groups. Everyone knows what that means.

"But you wrote it," the producer says. "The allegory is working, just as you suggested it would."

"I was dreaming of The Golden Bowl, or The Turn of the Screw, but this turned into Animal Farm," the girl says. "Well, we resemble Stalinist Russia, so that makes sense," the producer says. "Allegory is out of control," replies the young girl. "It's disingenuous. It's dangerous. Replacements replaced realities. We're helping people enjoy censorship. Others may use this to their political advantage. This can't go on."

But Turks would never let The Empire of Love go. Before censorship it was a placeholder; now it's essential. It is their refuge, the only show where talking heads don't praise the government or disingenuously criticise "certain aspects" of state power. It is a refuge from the politics-obsessed who dominate screens around the clock, seven days a week. The Empire of Love episodes drop every Sunday, and Turks relish cracking their secrets. It has become a Turkish Alice in Wonderland: a fantasy for those condemned to a nightmare.

"The genie is out of the bottle," the writer says. "Still, there is an antidote to allegory, and it is dystopia." She proposes a Turkish Chernobyl: transporting the trio to the catastrophic Turkey of 2023 – rat-infested, on fire, bankrupted, in a grinding civil war – may, in her view, help the show flourish for another season. "At least we'll have more agency."

The producer welcomes this appetite for change. He'll miss the piece of hay they injected to the show; but "replacement images", he agrees, threaten public order. The dystopia could be timeless: with no links to contemporary Turkey they may act more freely and disregard consequences of allegory. He hopes this will be a "renaissance", a "reboot" for The Empire of Love. Besides, they can sell branded merchandise.

They are sketching the plot as we speak. Imitation characters are imported from libraries of apocalyptic fiction. Mock conflicts between imaginary powers appear on blank pages. Cliches come to the rescue of a binge-worthy fifth season. Pencils are sharpened; volumes of Atwood, Bradbury and Zamyatin novels borrowed from library shelves. Much fine tuning lies ahead. Those who don't have to don't know it, but avoiding reality is really hard work.

Kaya Genç *is author of the recently released* The Lion and the Nightingale, *as well as* Under the Shadow *and* An Istanbul Anthology. *He is a contributing editor for Index on Censorship, based in Istanbul*

Playing the joker

Writer **Jonathan Tel** talks to **Rachael Jolley** about his love of jokes and what they say about different cultures

48(04): 86/92 | DOI: 10.1177/0306422019894894

LEFT: Jonathan Tel, whose story (right) on jokes in a Syrian prison is inspired by interviews he has done with Syrian refugees

"**JOKES ARE, OF** course, very often subversive. And I am somebody who collects jokes," said British short-story writer Jonathan Tel.

One of the inspirations for his latest tale, Old Jokes are the Worst, came from the Syrian refugees he is working with, and an academic course he is teaching in Germany.

Tel, who won the Sunday Times short-story prize in 2016, is in Berlin collecting material for his next project, and it is from there he speaks to Index on Censorship about the new short story that he wrote exclusively for this magazine.

Another part of the inspiration for this story is the power of humour in incredibly traumatic circumstances. Set among people in a prison in Damascus, Syria, and the jokes they tell, it also gives a sense of how some people keep going.

"Some of them are, indeed, inspired by jokes going around the Arab world for centuries," he said. "I am particularly interested in jokes from other cultures and other periods of history."

Tel is obviously interested in the power of humour and the differences and connections it can make. "If they find it funny and I didn't, what does that say about the differences in our cultures?"

In the past, many of Tel's stories have been set in China, including his prize-winning story The Human Phonograph, in which a woman is reunited with her geologist husband at a remote Chinese nuclear base in the early years of the Cultural Revolution. Tel has spent time in China and is clearly fascinated by it. Although he is not writing about it at the moment, he doesn't rule out featuring it in the future. He also has a book with a Chinese theme coming out in the USA in January called Scratching the Head of Chairman Mao.

Tel hasn't yet visited Syria, although he has travelled widely in the Middle East. But he is very interested in the country following his interactions with the Syrians he has met so far.

He is also intrigued by how the Syrian refugees in Germany and the Germans get on. "There can be mutual understanding and mutual misunderstandings," he said.

"The frame is pretty bleak because the situation is pretty bleak," said Tel of his decision to set the short story in a prison. But he talks about how it shows a window into this world, where there is laughter and people try to make their lives a little better by telling jokes. And he hopes that readers will feel that the prisoners are real and will see them as human beings.

People find some kind of freedom in a repressive society by telling jokes, adds Tel, referring to why the jokes are so important to the sense of place.

The prisoners in this story are so used to telling jokes that they don't even have to tell them any more, referring to them as just numbers and still understanding how they end. ⊗

Rachael Jolley is the editor-in-chief of Index on Censorship

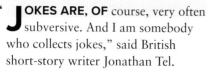

The frame is pretty bleak because the situation is pretty bleak

Old Jokes are the Worst

Jonathan Tel

PRISONERS IN A jail in Damascus are telling a joke about prisoners in a jail in Damascus.

A newcomer has just been thrown into the cell, his right arm broken, his legs in shackles – both in reality and in the joke.

*

'One of the old-timers calls out, "Forty-eight!" and the others laugh.

Somebody else shouts, "Thirty-seven!" Gales of laughter.

Another prisoner: "Twenty-nine!" Even more laughter and applause.

The newcomer asks what's going on, and it's explained: they've told their stock of jokes so many times they know them by heart, and have assigned them numbers on a list. No need to repeat the whole joke then, just the number.

The newcomer calls out, "Twenty-two!" Followed by silence. "How come nobody laughs?"

"It's the way you tell it."

*

The newcomer tries to smile, but he's in pain and, besides, he's heard the joke before.

"Twenty-two," he groans. "What kind of joke is that anyway?" And a skinny, almost skeletal, man answers him:

*

'Everybody was hungry.

'A woman said to her husband, "Go to the river. Maybe you can catch a fish."

'So the man put a worm on a hook, and he stood by the Euphrates. He stood there all morning, and he stood there all afternoon. He sang, "Come to me, fish! I invite you to my home!" Then he sang, "Come to me fish! You are guest of honour at my banquet!" Then he sang, "Come to me, fish! I will fry you in olive oil, and I will bite your crispy skin, and I will swallow your succulent flesh, and I will suck your bones, and I will crunch your head between my teeth!"

'It was almost sunset, and the man was about to give up. Just then, a fat fish took the bait, and the man reeled it in. He called out to his wife, "My darling, my dearest! Light a fire, and put oil in the pan. The guest of honour is on the way!"

'His wife called back, "What oil? There's no oil to be had for love or money anywhere in the village!"

'The man cursed, and he threw the fish back in the river.

'And the fish shouted, "Long live Bashar al-Assad!"

*

"I've heard this one before, too," the newcomer says.

The skinny man glares. "The joke's not over yet."

*

'The first person to tell the joke of The Patriotic Fish was arrested by the "ghost" police, and was never seen again.

'The next person to tell it was careful to whisper. All the same he was caught and executed.

'The third person didn't tell the whole joke; there was no need, since everybody knew it already.

And the fish in the Euphrates feasted on the jokesters. They leaped into the air, shouting, "Long live Bashar al-Assad!"

Instead he alluded to it by reciting the punchline, "Long live Bashar al-Assad!" He was buried in an unmarked grave.

'The subsequent tellers paraphrased the punchline. For example, they might say "Hurrah for Bashar al-Assad!" Or "Three cheers for Bashar al-Assad!" Or a slogan such as "Allah, Syria, Bashar, and nothing but!" The more they praised the President, the more they were mocking him. To be on the safe side, the police shot everyone in the village, and threw their bodies into the river.

'And the fish in the Euphrates feasted on the jokesters. They leaped into the air, shouting, "Long live Bashar al-Assad!".'

*

Silence. Somebody says, "When I first heard it, it was told about Bashar's father, Hafez al-Assad."

Another prisoner says, "I was living in Iraq, and they told the same joke about Saddam Hussein."

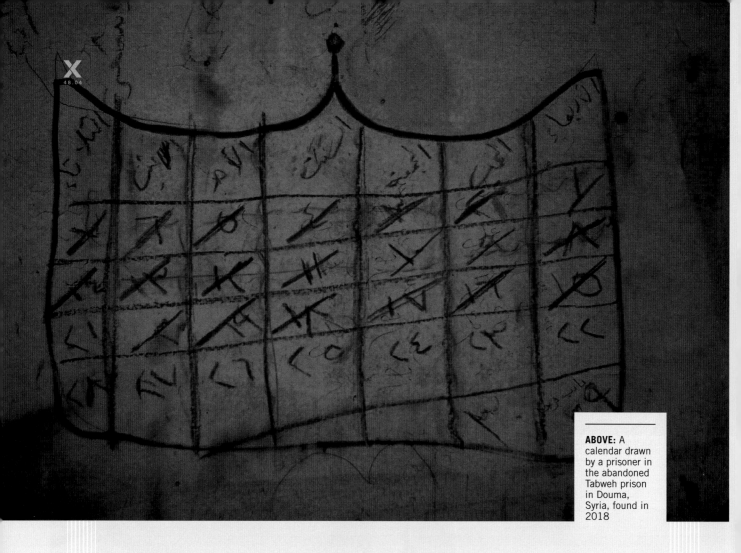

ABOVE: A calendar drawn by a prisoner in the abandoned Tabweh prison in Douma, Syria, found in 2018

→   An older man: "In Egypt, they told it about Abdul Gamal Nasser, and the fish weren't in the Euphrates, they were in the Nile. It probably goes back to the Pharaohs."

Silence resumes. Then the newcomer calls out, "Forty-eight!" and a prisoner with a thin moustache responds:

*

'Other people may have excised this from their memory, but I remember how thrilled we all were when Bashar al-Assad came to power. He was young, with a pretty wife, and he'd studied in the UK. He would bring our country into the modern world. He was an ophthalmologist. We weren't quite sure what an ophthalmologist does, but we knew he had looked into many eyes. "Allah, Syria, Bashar, and nothing but!" It was compulsory to chant this, but even if it hadn't been, we would have done it of our own free will.

'He had a thin moustache, a lisp, and a long neck. Many of us, too, cultivated a thin moustache, and affected a lisp, and tilted our chin up to make our neck seem longer. We'd be playing soccer with our pals, and it would seem there were eleven Bashars on the team.

'Then, as the leader became less popular, our moustaches thickened, and our lisps vanished, and our necks shrank. All except for Qusay. He'd had a lisp ever since he was an infant, his neck was naturally long, and his moustache refused to grow; it looked like a moth had settled on his lip.

Naturally we teased him. We used to tug his moustache playfully, and declare the old-fashioned oath, "I swear by my moustache!" And there was a Ramadan soap opera popular back then, set a century ago, about a man who stakes his moustache as bond. We taunted him, "Did you lose your moustache in a business dealing, ha ha!?"

'Qusay had enough of this. He told everybody he was going on holiday to Istanbul. When he came back, we realised he'd been to the moustache transplant clinic. He sported the kind of bushy moustache nicknamed a "Stalin". He looked like everybody's socialist uncle.

'So we played a prank on him. We pretended not to recognise him. "Who are you?"

"It's me! It's me, Qusay!"

"No, I don't know anybody of that name with a moustache like that. I never saw you before in my life!"

'A month later he vanished. We think he was taken away by the "ghost" police. No one knows what he was accused of, or his fate.'

*

A man in the corner hides behind his moustache, ignored by the others.

The newcomer tries, "Thirty-seven!" and a fellow with a bushy beard says, "That's the number of the joke I told the woman who was interrogating me when I applied for asylum in Berlin. Maybe that's why I was deported back here. The Germans have no sense of humour – any more than we do."

*

'We were in a dugout on the outskirts of Kobane, three kilometres from the front. The sun set and we prayed the *maghrib* prayer, and Fazel began to sing. Ah, you should have heard him! You'd think you were in *Jannah* already! He sang a name for Allah, and he sang another name for Allah … We have ninety-nine names for Allah; you have ninety-nine names for sausage …Then he sang a *nasheed* about the *hoor al-ayn*, "O my brothers, how I yearn to be with her!" He sang the beauty of the virgin who awaits him in *Jannah*, with her eyes like pearls and her skin so fair she is transparent. Finally, the APC rolled up, and Fazel raised one finger aloft to signal his allegiance to Islamic State, and he strapped the belt packed with explosives around his waist, and he was driven away toward the front.

'Then Jawdat took up the *nasheed*. Ah, you should have heard Jawdat! Maybe not such a pretty voice as Fazel's, but he held up a Coke bottle like a microphone, and he imitated a contestant on Arab Idol. He grinned at the audience and twisted his hips. He slapped his belly to keep the beat going. "O my brothers, how I yearn to be with her!" Then the APC came back again, and the sergeant fastened the explosives around Jawdat, and he too was driven away.

→   'So there were only two of us left, me and Alaeddin. Alaeddin began to sing. He sang the *nasheed* about the reward for the faithful, he sang about the beautiful *hoor al-ayn* waiting for him in *Jannah*, he sang like a tomcat bawling, he sang like a door creaking, he sang like fingernails scraping on a chalkboard, he sang like the screams of the *Kuffar* burning eternally in *Jahannam*. Alaeddin squeezed his eyes shut, the better to concentrate on his horrible *nasheed*. The only creature who could enjoy such a performance is a *Jinn*. He crept out of the darkness. To the *Jinn* it seemed this was the voice of his beloved, his *Jinna*, and she was singing of her love for him, her one true *Jinn*, for him alone. The *Jinn* crept closer and closer. He was ten metres tall when he stepped over the barbed wire, and he shrank to fit through the door frame, and he shrank even more so he could perch inside the ammo box on the floor between me and Alaeddin, and listen. "O my brothers, how I yearn to be with her!" I kicked the lid of the box shut.

'The sergeant grabbed Alaeddin, shoved him into the APC, and drove away.

'Me? No, I did not sing. I have no voice, and I know it. The *nasheed* continued only in my head, while the *Jinn* thrashed and battered inside the ammo box, begging to be let out. "I'll give you anything you desire, in return for my freedom!"

'I thought about all the places in this world and other worlds I could visit, all the fates that could be mine. It seemed ten thousand voices were singing, shouting, whispering, ululating, praising, cursing, begging to be heard. I picked the option which, I guess, most men in my situation would have chosen.

'"I'll let you go on condition you transport me instantly far from any battlefield. Put me in a warm, clean room in, let's say, Germany; and, while you're about it, give me four fifteen-year-old virgins with blonde hair and blue eyes, please!"'

'I could hear the *Jinn* inside the box counting on his fingers (they've got no thumbs, you know) fifteen times, and he promised to make my wish come true.

'"O my brothers, how I yearn to be with her!"

'And that's how I made it from Syria to Berlin, and how come I'm sitting here talking with you, a sixty-year-old virgin.'

※

The door opens, and guards drag the prisoners away, one by one. The newcomer is the last one left. He remains in the cell, locked up in solitary confinement. There he is, even now, while I'm writing this and you're reading this. He's shouting out numbers, and laughing, and laughing, and laughing.

....

Jonathan Tel *is a novelist and short-story writer. He has won Sunday Times and Commonwealth short-story prizes. He is currently based in Berlin*

ESSEX BOOK FESTIVAL

28 February - 29 March 2020
100 Events | 40 Venues
200 Writers & Artists

Brave New Worlds

From Climate Change to AI,
Protest and Dissent to Radical
Utopias, join us for a month of
challenging conversations,
adventurous writing
and dynamic debates
in over 40 venues
across Essex...

essexbookfestival.org.uk

Going graphic

Graphic novels can reach a wider audience than other types of journalism, **Andalusia Knoll Soloff** tells **Jessica Ní Mhainín**

48(04): 94/97 | DOI: 10.1177/0306422019894895

LEFT: Andalusia Knoll Soloff and Marco Parra

JOURNALIST ANDALUSIA KNOLL Soloff was reporting on the enforced disappearance of 43 students in Mexico when she realised that her news stories were not reaching as wide an audience as they should.

"A 1,500-word article or a two-minute video could not communicate the families' profound sense of loss, pain and anxiety," she said.

She had been living alongside the students' families and knew that the stories needed to be told in full, so she began to see the power of graphic novels.

In the graphic novelette They Are Killing Us, published by Index for the first time here, Knoll Soloff and illustrator Marco Parra commemorate some of Mexico's murdered journalists and demonstrate the ongoing risks facing journalists there.

"Every year, more journalists are forcibly 'disappeared' and murdered, and their cases are not solved," Knoll Soloff said. "People think that Mexico is just violent because of organised crime, but there's a whole system of collusion between the government and organised crime that enables journalists to be killed.

"We thought that things would improve now that there is a new, more progressive president, but many of the journalists who are killed are working in small isolated places, where the federal government has been unable to effect change," she said. "Journalists have to be advocates for their own safety. Being in solidarity with your colleagues is not just an option – it's a necessity."

Knoll Soloff, who is originally from the USA and works as a reporter in Mexico for Al-Jazeera, among others, added: "As a teenager, I used to love reading graphic novels. I learned about things, such as the war in the Balkans, that I would never have known about if they were not in that format."

The ability of the graphic novel to make complicated issues more accessible is one of the reasons why she also decided to work on a book about the 43 missing students from the Ayotzinapa teaching college, who in 2014 were detained by police and then "disappeared".

Her upcoming book, Vivos se los Llevaron (Taken Alive), which was published in Spanish this November, follows the students' parents as they search for their sons. Knoll Soloff said relating individual stories without being repetitive would have been difficult if not for the graphic novel format.

When the parents visited towns in the state of Guerrero to gather support and put pressure on the government, people came out in their thousands. She said she could show that support in the faces of the people in the drawings.

The case of the Ayotzinapa students has come to represent the difficulty faced by Mexico's lower social strata to have their voices heard. "Some of the parents are partially illiterate," she said. "When reports were published about the investigation, they would not read them – they were 400 pages of text. But they [can] read the graphic version."

As well as being one of Mexico's poorest states, Guerrero has one of the highest rates of violence – including against journalists. "Being a journalist in Guerrero is how I got involved in press freedom issues," said Knoll Soloff. "I often report on the same issues that journalists [who] have been murdered, or at least threatened or harassed, report on." ⊗

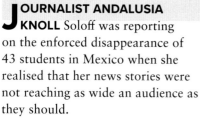

There's a whole system of collusion between the government and organised crime that enables journalists to be killed

Jessica Ní Mhainín is a policy and advocacy officer at Index on Censorship

THEY ARE KILLING US- ANDALUSIA K. SOLOFF & MARCO PARRA

"In Mexico it is more dangerous to investigate a murder than commit one."- John Gibler

JAVIER VALDEZ
CULIACAN, SINALOA
15.05.2017

MARISOL MACIAS
NUEVO LAREDO, TAMAULIPAS
24.09.2011

NEVITH CONDES
TEJUPILCO, MEXICO STATE
24.08.2019

MARIO GOMEZ
YAJALON, CHIAPAS
21.09.2018

Since 2000, 131 journalists have been murdered in Mexico according to the press freedom group Article 19. In this same time frame, 24 journalists have been disappeared.

The majority worked for local outlets, often focusing on covering the close ties between the government and criminal organisations.

- Mario worked for a local newspaper, El Heraldo, and had previously denounced threats against his life. He was shot and killed as he left his house. His colleagues continue to demand a proper investigation.

- Nevith founded the online portal, Observatorio del Sur so he could "share the microphone with people that feel that their rights have been violated". He had received threats and was stabbed to death. Hundreds honoured him at his funeral.

- Javier was an investigative reporter who founded the local newspaper, RioDoce. He was shot in broad daylight, blocks from the newspaper.

- Marisol worked at a local paper and published on social networks about criminal activity in the region. Her decapitated body was found with a keyboard, headphones and the note "I am here because of my reporting."

99 percent of crimes against journalists go unpunished.

Crime scenes and forensic evidence are not properly preserved.

The intellectual authors are rarely prosecuted.

Regina Martínez was an investigative reporter in Xalapa, Veracruz with the Mexican weekly magazine Proceso. She investigated the rape and death of an indigenous elder, Ernestina Ascencio, at the hands of soldiers. On 28 April 2012 she was murdered in her own home.

The government declared her death unrelated to her journalism and called it a crime of passion. They said she might have been killed by a lover based on the fact that she had makeup in her house. The reporters who investigated her murder received threats and the real suspects of the crime were never prosecuted.

EXIGIMOS QUE EL MUNICIPIO...

Moisés Sánchez published his own local newspaper, La Union, in Medellin, Veracruz. In 2015 following threats from the town mayor, he was kidnapped in front of his family and disappeared. His body was later found on the side of the road.

The government once again declared that he was not killed for journalism, since he was also a taxi driver. Three years after his death two policemen were arrested, but the mayor who is believed to be the actual criminal roams free. His son keeps the newspaper La Union alive.

The Mexican Government has a special program dedicated to protecting journalists and human rights defenders, that helps them relocate and even gives them panic buttons...

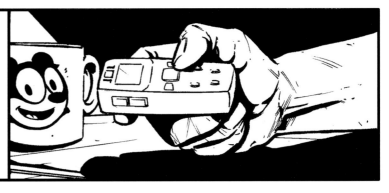

and bodyguards. But unfortunately, these measures have been proven ineffective and one journalist has been murdered while under the protection of this government programme.

Realising that the state is incapable of guaranteeing freedom of expression, journalists in Mexico build networks to support and protect each other.

When the government failed to investigate the murder of reporter Miroslava Breach, journalists formed their own investigative team and launched proyectomiroslava.org

Every time a journalist is assassinated in Mexico, their colleagues take to the streets and demand an end to the violence. You can kill the messenger, but you can't kill the truth.

Andalusia Knoll Soloff is a freelance journalist and **Marco Parra** is an illustrator. They are both based in Mexico

INDEX AROUND THE WORLD

Governments seek to control reports

Terrorism allegations and journalists' safety were two of the issues tackled by Index during the past quarter, reports **Orna Herr**

48(04): 98/100 I DOI: 10.1177/0306422019894896

"**J**OURNALISTS CAN FACE** pressure from regimes to write disinformation, or threats from thugs supporting a certain party. That can be a really big threat around election times," said Index advocacy director Joy Hyvarinen, who was part of a recent discussion on the theme in London. "There is really a need to make people more media literate so that they are more critical and don't just accept what they've been told," she said after the event organised by the Carter Centre and Hacks/ Hackers at Asia House. Hyvarinen added that safety for journalists around election times was a high priority.

The way information is shared online was also debated in October when Index partnered with human rights organisation Liberty at a fringe event held by the UK's Conservative party at its annual conference. Hyvarinen, who was a panellist, said the discussion focused on threats and challenges to freedom of expression online. She argued that the government's Online Harms proposals would cause a new set of problems. The draft legislation, outlined in April, introduced the idea of companies having a duty of care in terms of what appears on their websites, but Hyvarinen said: "It is a really badly thought through idea." Senior managers could face fines or even jail but Hyvarinen

suggested that, in an effort to be seen to be "doing something" about issues such as the spread of terrorist content, the legislation could penalise people who were not to blame. She said: "It's important to note that duty of care and all these sanctions … don't apply just to the big social media platform providers, they apply to everyone according to this proposal. Small companies – start-ups, for example – could be liable for things that they do not have the resources to avoid or control, so that's hugely worrying."

Jessica Ní Mhainín, policy research and advocacy officer, who is managing the Index media monitoring project, said: "Independent journalists, who have been writing about the Turkish incursion into Kurdish-held areas of northern Syria, even just on their social media pages, are being targeted for using words such as 'warfare', 'incursion' and 'invasion'."

Press freedom in Turkey has been steadily declining under President Recep Tayyip Erdogan. Turkey is now the world's biggest jailer of journalists, according to Reporters Without Borders, with more than 200 arrested or detained under charges relating to their work since the failed coup in July 2016. Ní Mhainín said the incursion into Syria posed the most recent threat to journalists, as they struggle to report military activity objectively.

After the coup attempt, Erdogan declared a state of emergency and took draconian action against the media. The state of emergency officially ended in July 2018 but Ní Mhainín said: "Since many emergency laws were transposed into state law, the ending of the state of emergency has made little difference to civil liberties, including media freedom, in Turkey." An Index report focusing on media freedom in Turkey in May and June 2019 found a surge in physical attacks on journalists.

Ní Mhainín is now working on another report tracking attacks on media freedom in Turkey between April and November 2019. Reporting trends show that journalists are being charged with offences related to terrorism and insulting media officials. The risk increases if journalists show support for, or affiliation

with, the Kurds. "If you're saying anything in favour of the Kurds, they will arrest you and put you in jail, [and assume] you are part of a terrorist organisation," she said.

Author Kaya Genç, who is the magazine's contributing editor in Turkey, told Index that journalists often did not speak out against issues surrounding the Kurds or defend those who do. "That kind of solidarity, you don't see it in Turkey because people don't want to lose their jobs," he said. Erdogan has cultivated an atmosphere of fear – the result of an assault on freedom of expression and a culture of disinformation. The Turkish government's attempts to frame the incursion into Syria as a peaceful mission could be categorised as the latter.

Inaya Folarin Iman, manager of the Free Speech Is For Me project at Index, spoke at the Battle of Ideas Festival held at the Barbican Centre, London, in November. On the panel – Is a New Far-Right on the Rise in Europe?

– Folarin Iman argued that the UK government was trying to exploit public concern about the far right "in order to sink their tentacles deeper into tech companies, and essentially increase censorship and online regulation". At the same time, she argued that those who were expressing anti-immigration views could face pressure not to speak, which could be a free-speech issue, too. She said the term "far-right … is essentially being used as a tool to demonise political opponents, particularly people that might have criticisms of mass immigration".

ABOVE: Chinese cartoonist Badiucao waves his Lennon flag at the screening for the film about him, China's Artful Dissident at the Tate Exchange, London

An Index report focusing on media freedom in Turkey in May and June 2019 found a surge in physical attacks on journalists

LIBERTY
STAND
UP TO
POWER

ABOVE: A panel at the fringe event at the Conservative party conference. Left to right, Joy Hyvarinen, journalist Katy Balls, Liberty's Martha Spurrier and John Whittingdale MP

→ Also at the Battle of Ideas, Index CEO Jodie Ginsberg brought her concerns about the direction of freedom of expression online to a panel about privacy. In response to concerns that there was not sufficient online protection, Ginsberg said: "We have plenty of legislation that deals with explicit threats of violence against women, and against men. What worries me is that people are seeing this kind of unpleasant narrative and saying the solution to that is to prevent those people from speaking at all, to ban and censor that language. If we feel that there are certain subjects that are essentially off-limits because we are being watched for what we say about them, that fundamentally alters the public political discourse."

The fight for free political discourse in a hostile climate was the dominant theme of the evening when Index, in partnership with the Tate Exchange, hosted a screening in October of China's Artful Dissident, by filmmaker Danny Ben-Moshe. The documentary follows Badiucao, a Chinese cartoonist who fled to Australia, whose work is critical of President Xi Jinping's government. Most recently he created work to demonstrate his solidarity with the

protesters in Hong Kong. He was at the screening, and spoke of the importance of freedom of expression on social media. He said: "There is a relatively large community on Twitter from mainland China – about one million people. These are the people who will see my work, will download my work, will repost [it] inside China." News that circulates in mainland China from Hong Kong is closely monitored and filtered, so the sharing of work such as Badiucao's is of critical importance to combat a one-sided government narrative.

Index editor-in-chief Rachael Jolley attended a roundtable at the Institute for Human Sciences in Vienna in conjunction with the Vienna Humanities Festival. One key discussion was about those in power trying to control narratives about history. Jolley said: "The control of history is a way of disinforming people – it's a way of deliberately giving people inaccurate information. You're seeing it in lots of different countries … national leaders like to portray a history that falls in line with their view of the world or the world they're trying to promote."

Promotion of a certain version of history can be used for political gains. Jolley cited Canadian historian Margaret MacMillan, a past Index contributor. MacMillan had described how a country's history can be manipulated by a government to form a particular national identity and then draw support for its agenda. Jolley said the rewriting of history often presented an idealistic version of the past, and "that sort of rose-tinted idealism of a nostalgic past is used to portray a certain type of politics that is quite often anti-immigrant and anti-modernisation".

Finally, Index's year-long training and mentorship programme empowering people to defend their right to free speech has just begun. Seven people from the UK and six in the USA will be offered mentoring and media training in order to gain confidence to publicly discuss the importance of freedom of expression. ⊗

Orna Herr is Index's editorial assistant and the Liverpool John Moores University/Tim Hetherington fellow for 2019-20

The control of history is a way of disinforming people – it's a way of deliberately giving people inaccurate information. You're seeing it in lots of different countries

END NOTE

Culture vultures

Once targeted by dictatorships, theatres and galleries are now under political pressure to close shows in democracies, too. **Jemimah Steinfeld** reports

48(04): 101/104 I DOI: 10.1177/0306422019894898

THE CANCELLATION OF the Billy Elliot musical in Hungary; a ban on political discussions at a theatre in Freiberg, Germany; an investigation into producers of a play about child abuse in the Catholic church in Poland – such is the state of the arts today, with anecdotes of harassment and censorship becoming widespread. As far-right groups gain momentum around the world, they've got their sights not only on seats in government but also on seats at the theatre.

The latest victim of the trend is Germany, where anti-immigration party Alternative for Germany (AfD) is going after shows and exhibitions. Marc Jongen, unofficial party philosopher of the AfD, has said he wants to "de-grime the [left-dominated] cultural scene", while Hans-Thomas Tillschneider, another

---

As far-right groups gain momentum around the world, they've got their sights not only on seats in government but also on seats at the theatre

senior member, has called for theatres to return to a traditional repertoire.

Index spoke to Marc-Oliver Hendriks, executive director of the opera house Staatstheater Stuttgart, who said this summer an AfD politician requested the nationalities of the members of those employed in publicly funded theatres in the state, which included theirs (the ministry responded by providing the number of international artists, not their exact nationality). The ministry also made "a statement on how the arts have always been international and that the overruling aspect of employment is artistic excellence".

With incidents like this becoming more commonplace, the Mobile Council against Right-Wing Extremism, who provide advice for those dealing with right-wing extremist intimidation and threats in Germany, recently published a handbook for cultural institutions and artists on how to navigate the rise of the far right. It advises people to stay calm, to know of and agree on institutional values and to make these known.

"Public statements on one's own democratic stance are particularly effective if they are made in conjunction with other cultural institutions and associations. The strength lies in the diversity of the rejections of right-wing attacks on artistic freedom and the cultural sector," Hamid Mohseni from the Council told Index.

"There is pressure on cultural institutions – mainly in eastern Germany but not only in eastern Germany – from the AfD and their allies on the extremist far right. This alliance and the threat that stems from it is very different from the situation 10 years ago," said Roman Schmidt, who is head of the contemporary history division of the Heinrich Böll Foundation, a think-tank that works on democracy and human rights.

Schmidt says right now the power of the AfD is curtailed as it is not in government, but he's worried that it could gain control at the *Lander* (state) or municipal level. "This would be a disaster for Germany because when it comes to cultural and educational institutions, the *Lander* have the say and the budget."

Schmidt, who has a doctorate in history, →

added: "We have a strong polarisation between a liberal, predominantly urban part of the population that has a cosmopolitan, pluralist outlook and a more nationalist, closed, inward-looking part." He points out that in the Weimar Republic the arts flourished, but what happened next showed how democracies can fail very quickly.

In Brazil, this polarisation is particularly

SEVEN SWIPES AT ART CENSORSHIP, AND A RESPONSE

||||||||||||||||||||||||||||||||||||||||||||||||||

THE FAR-RIGHT ALTERNATIVE for Germany (AfD) party's attempts to stiffle cultural freedom in Germany are prolific. Here's just some of the arts it took aim at:

- In 2017, an AfD politician in Aachen threatened theatre director Reza Jafari with legal action unless he altered his play to omit parallels between right-wing populism and fanatical Islam.
- In Paderborn, the AfD filed a defamation claim against the city's theatre over an illustration on a flyer that compared the AfD's rise to that of the Nazi party.
- In Berlin, the AfD has filed several legal complaints against an exhibition on far-right extremism that referenced the AfD.
- Political events were banned at the central theatre in Freiberg following complaints from an AfD councillor, who labelled a book reading and discussion on right-wing populism as "left-green ideology".
- In Dresden, which declared a "Nazi emergency" this November, AfD members took part in protests in 2017 against a public art installation by the Syrian-German artist Manaf Halbouni. One AfD politician said the installation was a "monument to the sharia state".
- A public sculpture in Kassel called Monument for Strangers and Refugees was labelled *entstellende Kunst* ("disfiguring art") by the AfD. It was relocated from the main square in 2018.
- This summer, in Stuttgart, an AfD politician requested a list of the original nationalities of all artists in state-run opera, orchestra and ballet companies.
- One fightback: The Cinexx cinema in Hachenburg offered free admission to screenings of Schindler's List this January for all AfD members. The ticket offer was provoked by comments from the AfD which included referring to the Holocaust memorial in Berlin as "a monument of shame".

pronounced. The country legalised same-sex marriage in 2013 but it is also one of the most dangerous places to be LGBT in the world. The young, urban and educated are pitted against the religious and conservatives. In President Jair Bolsonaro, the latter group have found an ally.

Since coming to power on 1 January, Bolsonaro has made cleansing the arts a central goal. Of his many threats, he's called for Ancine, Brazil's state-backed film agency, to accept "filters" or face closure. He accused the agency of supporting "pornography" – a reference to its co-financing of Bruna Surfistinha, a drama based on the real-life story of a middle-class prostitute.

Performer, choreographer and writer Wagner Schwartz is feeling the sting. Even before Bolsonaro came to power, back in 2017 Schwartz found himself at the centre of a storm following his performance of La Bête – a one-man show in which he lay naked at the Museum of Modern Art in São Paulo and invited people to move parts of his body. When a four-year-old innocently did (and it was recorded), allegations of paedophilia spread like wildfire online.

"As soon as I was called a 'paedophile' by the extreme right at the end of 2017, [getting] work in some Brazilian institutions became harder. In 2018, for instance, only local and independent festivals decided to programme my work. I'm still censored today."

Schwartz says the major institutions want to avoid scandals and political problems, something Index picked up on when contacting Ancine. The agency was keen to state that it would not comment on anything political following our questions about Bolsonaro.

Scottish playwright Jo Clifford sounds an even more alarming tone. "Since Bolsonaro has

CREDIT: Mauro Pimentel/Getty

come into power it has become too dangerous to perform in Brazil," she said of her play The Gospel According to Jesus, Queen of Heaven, which features Jesus as a trans woman. The play was on tour in Brazil until recently.

"The last time they did so, a bomb was thrown into the performance space and armed police invaded the theatre. They performed anyway, but it was clear that to continue [after that] would be at too great a cost."

When The Gospel According to Jesus, Queen of Heaven was first performed, at Glasgow's Tron Theatre in 2009, there was a huge number of protests and calls for its ban.

Clifford has just completed a hugely successful 10th-anniversary festival of the play back at the Tron without protests. But last Christmas there was a run at Edinburgh's Traverse Theatre and an online petition demanding the play be banned attracted 24,674 signatures.

"We are on the front line of a culture war that will only deepen and strengthen as the ecological and financial crisis worsens and the right feel more fearfully they are losing their grip on power," Clifford said.

Dóra Papp knows what that feels like. In

Viktor Orbán's nationalist Hungary, "liberalism" has long been a dirty word. Since his most recent election win last year, the Fidesz party leader has upped the ante, pledging to "embed the political system in a cultural era". That has translated into funds being cut from the arts, on top of shows and talks being cancelled and newspaper editorials criticising plays as "promoting communism" or "gay propaganda".

Papp, who is an activist and former chief executive of an independent theatre company, appears exhausted by it all when we speak. She says that independent companies are suffering more and more, and that self-censorship is becoming rife in what was a once thriving cultural scene.

"Should they have confrontational subjects on their programmes or should they self-censor and try to get government funding?" she asked.

Papp also points out an irony about Orbán. As a result of Hungary's membership of the EU, artistic talent is draining out of the country. Freedom of movement – something that Orbán despises – is actually helping him when it comes to the arts.

"Even in those times there was a pressure to find a way to create something in

ABOVE: Director Artur Luanda Ribeiro prepares backstage for the premiere of Irmaos de Sangue at a theatre in Rio de Janeiro, Brazil this September. LGBT productions have been in the firing line since Bolosonaro took over

of Schindler's List in January in response to the AfD's disdain for Germany's focus on Holocaust remembrance. Theatres and other cultural institutions have also formed a network to ensure they show a united front. "It's a good reaction to what is happening," said Schmidt. "It's more important right now to work with as many people as possible, not just with your tribe."

→ Hungary," said Papp of Soviet-ruled Hungary. "But this is not a need now in Hungary. People facing problems have the opportunity to leave, and that has a bad effect on willingness to change."

When it's not about attacking the arts, it's about supplanting them. Bolsonaro is clear on his vision for the director's chair. He wants art to be about "Brazilian heroes". In Croatia, it's folklore. Miljenka Buljevic, manager of literary centre Booksa in Zagreb, says that when Croatia was applying to become an EU country, the country outwardly committed to liberal values.

"But now that we are in the EU, we have conservatives in power and folklore societies have embraced certain discourse. All of a sudden, people are embracing folklore," she told Index.

Buljevic is upset about the recent closure of the last independent cinema in Zagreb. In its place stands a shopping mall. "The ecosystem is falling apart. We see more and more commercial things," she said. Buljevic does point to some positives. The founding of Kultura Nova in 2011 marked a turning point for the arts in the country, with its aim of "improving the system of financing the arts and culture", and her organisation has recently doubled in size.

And the backlash is being met by a counter-backlash. Back in Germany, the Cinexx cinema in the historic town of Hachenburg offered members of the AfD free tickets to a screening

Perhaps the most successful counter-offensive has come from a Brazilian federal judge. In August, Bolsonaro took away nearly $17 million in film grants from about 80 movies, including films with LGBT content. In October, judge Laura Carvalho ruled against this move. "Freedom of expression, equality and non-discrimination deserve the protection of the judiciary," she said at the time.

Director Emerson Maranhão, whose documentary Transversais, about the lives of transgender people in Brazil, was targeted, told Reuters that while the fight was not over yet (the government can still appeal the decision), justice had been done. "We are living in lonely times, but decisions like this make me feel like we are back to living in a democracy."

For Schwartz, festival directors who are also affected by the situation in Brazil have supported him and work continues to come in. "I owe it to them," he said.

As for Buljevic, the best form of resistance is existence. She said: "I'm stubborn. I've been saying that ever since we started survival is the ultimate subversive strategy." ⊗

Jemimah Steinfeld is deputy editor at *Index on Censorship*